IT'S BEEN GREAT!

REBECCA LUKENS

It's Been Great!

By Rebecca Lukens

Editing and Proofreading by Steven Bauer

Cover and book design by Dave Bricker

❧ IT'S BEEN GREAT! ❧

For my children and theirs...

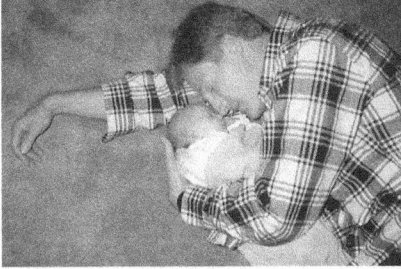

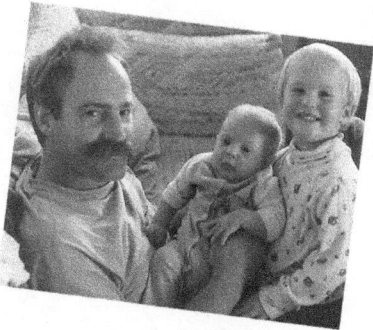

Rebecca Lukens

Oh, the memoir. You feel like a sucker these days for even picking one up. You read defensively, suspiciously. The minute you feel a twinge of empathy, doubt kicks in: Am I being conned? Is this just another pack of half-truths or outright confabulations? ... Memoirs are, by their nature, solipsistic affairs. There's no getting around it. But there is a point at which a writer gets stuck so deep in his own mind that the reader stops trusting. . . .

—Hugo Lindgren, New York *Times Book Review,* June 8, 2008

◙ Table of Contents ◙

Rebecca Lukens

❦ Preface ❦

Over the years I have been writing bits of memory for our writing group here at the Knolls. In 2010 I had an inspiration: Why not gather them into a paperback book for the family—for my children and theirs?

Suddenly, in my computer ineptitude, I lost it all.

At the Mac Shop they just shook their heads about retrieving my memoir. At Miami, daughter Sally found a skillful student who retrieved "everything," and with great delight I paid him and checked a number of entries to see if all was as it had been when I had finished, proofread, and saved it. As far as I could tell, it was, as they say, "good to go." Off to the printers.

Only when I had proudly mailed off copies to four children and six grandchildren did I settle down to read all of it. It was loaded with problems: double punctuation, word omissions, misplaced paragraphs, even garbled language. I was shocked. And embarrassed.

I therefore offer this new book, including the corrections and a second part, *Marginalia.* This volume includes the bits written since the first fiasco.

Please recycle the earlier mess.

~M

Rebecca Lukens

✤ Summer in Fargo ✤

As for summer, it was something else. When Fargo first heard about air pollution and was told not to burn leaves, or lake cottagers in Minnesota not to burn their garbage, natives were incredulous. Smoke pollutes the atmosphere? All that atmosphere? How could it? The sky was enormous. If the earth's curvature didn't interfere, it was so clear you might see Idaho. Or even The Coast. No mere leaf fire could pollute so vast a sky.

The night sky stretched endlessly, revealing the pinpricks of stars in the velvet dome, or rippled and flashed with the summer blues, greens, and golds of the Northern Lights. Some summer days the air shimmered with 90 plus heat, blurring the outlines of gabled farmhouses and private groves of trees.

During the drought, hot days dried the yard, leaving only dust and weeds. A few drops of rain left little volcano craters in the dust. When storm clouds gathered, Dad would look out across the fields, and say enviously, "It's raining in Casselton. I hope we get some." Sometimes the distance and speed of a faraway storm could be predicted, and farmers might work double-time to finish the haying or harvesting as the wind and rain rushed toward us.

The endless sky was endlessly under scrutiny, and for good reason. When our farm cousins saw a distant threatening blackness or a cloud funnel, they sought safety in the basement. "Tornado!"

or "Storm!" they'd shout to each other. They knew what a mighty wind could do: Once such a wind picked up Uncle Louie's garage and turned it around 180 degrees; their driveway then led to the blank back wall of the garage. At their home in Hannaford, a tornado might flatten wheat and barley fields so they couldn't be harvested. And if no tornado roared in, hail might beat the grain to sodden uselessness. We heard such stories from Dad's friend Oscar, a "hail adjustor" for an insurance company; he assessed damage for insured farmers.

In summer we went to "The Lakes" in Ottertail County, fifty miles into Minnesota. Threading our way over winding gravel roads between lakes to find Lake Lida or Prairie Lake, we'd then stop at the chosen place. In earlier days it was picnic time on a table-cloth spread on the sandy beach. Mother told us about the long trek of eight miles by horse and buggy or Model T from Pelican Rapids to picnic and swim at that beach. We snickered at pictures of what she called her bathing suit, a total cover-up with sleeves! Or we marveled at the pictures of Mom and her women friends who seemed to enjoy tame wading in the shallow water, fully dressed and holding up their long skirts to mid-calf, still wearing their elaborate hats pinned to elaborate whirls of hair, all to ward off the sun.

When I was a child our destination was sometimes Uncle Carl's cottage set back among the trees on Crystal Lake across from Lake

Lida, known for wall-eyed pike. For the three of us, it was exciting but not perfect. Fish might like the reedy shoreline and squishy
bottom of Crystal, but even with the lo-o-ong dock stretching out
past the reeds, swimming in Crystal wasn't great for those of us
who had to keep feet on the bottom.

One summer Dad knocked together a raft that floated on oil
drums. We'd swim out to it, scramble on and sun ourselves. Good
divers dove off into the over-my-head water. Once, when sister
Ruthie left her prized birthday watch on the raft so as not to get
it wet, it slipped overboard. Horrified, she dove for it time after
time, frightening us all with the possibility of her drowning from
exhaustion. As she groped in the dark reaches, her fingers caught
the bracelet circle and she sputtered to the surface, triumphantly
waving the watch.

On the Fourth we were often at the lake for fireworks. All around
the shoreline we could see the bright streaks of skyrockets sent
out over the water from other cottages. Dad not only aimed our
rockets out over the water, but made us aim the popping Roman
candles there, too. We made figure eights in the air with the fizzing
sparklers, or touched with the glowing punk a whole pack of lady-
fingers to set them cracking and snapping. Bob had bigger ideas.
Round cherry bombs would blow a tin can in the air, and really fat
crackers sounded like gunfire. "Throw them way out, Bob, way out!"
No one was hurt. We'd been carefully trained.

At home in Fargo there were devils-on-the-walk, flat devices that crackled and sparked and popped when crunched between our heels and the cement walk. The final event was the pinwheel tacked to a tree, whirring and whirling and throwing off multi-colored sparks to conclude the show.

In summer on busy Thirteenth Street, near the North Dakota Agricultural College, we heard the streetcar go by times and times a day. A waker-upper when we first moved there, the sound soon became so familiar we slept through it. When we grew brazen and heard the streetcar coming, we'd rush into the street to put a penny on the track. After the trolley run, we'd claim a flattened copper piece. Or we'd put two crossed straight pins—we called them common pins—on the track, retrieving them later as immovable scissors, heads enlarged to resemble handles and shafts flattened for blades.

At home on Fourth Street a year later, I joined the neighborhood kids playing "Red Rover, Red Rover come over," or "Beckon-beckon who's got the beckon." Under the streetlight we watched the circling bats—more likely swallows—out to catch insects attracted by the light. We captured a few bugs ourselves to put in Mason jars. In fact when we reached high school and had to make bug collections and identify them for biology class, we knew that under the streetlight was the place to start.

Late in his life, Dad, who had grown up on a North Dakota farm and had lived all his professional life in Fargo, said to each of us, "You should retire here. It's a great place to live: Unlike the South, we have a real change of seasons [minus 30 to plus 90]. We have an expressway going north and south [straight north to Winnipeg or south to Wahpeton]. And another going east and west [on to Mecca: Dickinson or St. Cloud]." Memories of the January that averaged minus 19 degrees chilled any latent interest.

But fry-eggs-on-the-sidewalk hot, or paralysis cold, North Dakota was good for children. Growing up was no hardship.

❧ Dad's Career Change ❧

With a wife and three children to support, Dad began a new career. He went to night school at the St. Paul College of Law, while during the day he was high school principal in North St. Paul—at a salary of $1800. (I know that because when I was hired to teach at St. Olaf College in 1947, I excitedly told him I was earning $2400 a year; he marveled at such generosity.)

Dad drove several nights a week—I think—to St. Paul, a drive of perhaps half an hour. He had to study after school and on weekends. More than once my screams at the teasing injustice meted out to me by my brother Bob meant I was shushed. Unhappy, I occasionally sat quietly on the toy box in the kitchen window, watching my friends play outside while I learned to be quiet. Sometimes during our unbearable racket, Dad left the house to study in the car.

When I was almost six, I got scarlet fever. A big red quarantine sign went up on the door, and Dad couldn't so much as peek in on me. Then Bob caught it, and Mom went into labor for my sister's coming birth. Mom was in Fairview Hospital, Bob and I went to Anchor Hospital for Contagious Diseases in St. Paul, and Dad packed to go to Bismarck, to take the North Dakota bar exam. Mom, of course, couldn't come see us. By way of kindly nurses, Bob and I sent printed notes to each other down the hospital hall. Dad, soon back from Bismarck, came to see us, bringing what we'd requested: figs for Bob and dates for me. He had to stand in the doorway of my room to be safe. We talked, and then he went down the hall to talk through the doorway to Bob. Christmas, my sixth birthday, and New Year's passed.

Rather than leave his job, Dad stayed on in the school system as superintendent. But he was eager to get on with his delayed career, and we soon moved to Fargo. As he checked the attorneys' offices in Fargo, he met Pete Garborg, a witty man who always made us laugh. He took Dad into his office to manage his practice when he was busy in the North Dakota legislature. Dad, not busy on his own yet, was very efficient, and soon a wealthy client named Lars Christianson offered Dad a retainer to handle all his business. I overheard parental discussions: "His income is from a liquor store. Are you sure you want to ally yourself with...." But it was a break impossible to refuse. Money was still tight, however, and I remember Dad telling Mom that for lunch he'd had just coffee and a piece of pie at Herbst Department Store. That sounded good to me, but Mom thought it inadequate. But she knew that Dad, who had borrowed on his life insurance policy, had no money.

Dad's college roommate lived across the street from us on Fourth Street and had a salaried job with the Chevrolet Company. I overheard Mom tell Dad, "When Alice Steen invited me to go shopping with her, I said I couldn't afford it. And Alice said, 'If I hear one more time that you can't afford it—'." The implied threat was that there would be no more invitations.

It wasn't long before Dad was making five dollars a week teaching a night class in Norwegian at North Dakota Agricultural College. Then he was appointed to the board of Fargo Savings and Loan, and each month came home with an extra ten dollars. But best of all was news that the Norwegian Consul in Minneapolis needed a Norwegian-speaking attorney to serve as Vice Consul for North Dakota. Dad was appointed, and began his duties serving North Dakota heirs to property in Norway, and the reverse. When he was asked what being Vice Consul for Norway out in North Dakota meant, he'd say he represented all the shipwrecked sailors of Norwegian extraction.

A popular speaker for national holidays, Dad now also spoke in Norwegian at the annual picnic celebrating Norwegian Independence Day, the seventeenth of May, the date of Norway's independence from Sweden. We three kids always went to the annual picnic but understood nothing he said.

During the War, Dad was active in relief efforts for the people of Norway who with their small army of about a thousand men were fighting the Nazi takeover. During the War, he was also state host to Crown Prince Olav and Princess Martha, as well as for Karl Hambro, the Prime Minister. After the War, Dad and Mom sailed to Oslo where Dad was knighted by King Haakon. At Dad's death, Bob dreamed of a hereditary knighthood, but it was not to be.

▦ Consumer Report ▦

The following treatments for freckle removal have been found to be ineffective:

1. Freckle cream
2. Buttermilk
3. Vinegar, hot or cold
4. Fermented watermelon juice

If you live long enough, your freckles will spread to join one another for an even tan.

Rebecca Lukens

Mom, Who Never Knew

I read once that all children think their parents are beautiful. So it's no surprise when I say that my mother was beautiful.

She didn't think so, and would protest quietly, "Oh, no. I have a Roman nose." It was her hair that I loved most. It was a great cloud around her head, soft brown, wavy, with what we would today call lots of "body." I think she held it in a soft bun, perhaps with big plastic hairpins and little wire ones. I remember such hairpins, and they were probably hers. Or perhaps my grandmother's.

When I was in the third grade, we moved to Fargo, and I remember some neighbor girls saying to me, "Gee, your mom is old." Suddenly I looked at mom and saw that her beautiful hair was turning gray. She had a wide swath of white just to the right of her center part. I hadn't ever looked at it that way. All I knew was that she was beautiful.

And at that point, I think I may have decided I was never going to get old so that my children would never be reminded of it. As the years went by, Mom's hair grew whiter and whiter, but it still was soft and cloudlike. She told me that as a little girl she'd worn her hair pulled back in braids, and that her mother thought them too pretty when the hairs slipped defiantly out of their elastics.

Mom rarely raised her voice to us, never to threaten or scold. I just knew I wanted to please her. She wasn't a tall woman, but she was trim and active. Once in a great while, I would hear Dad tease her about getting a little heavy, but I could never see it. She must have dreaded turning forty, because for her birthday Dad gave her a popular book called *Life Begins at Forty*. She just smiled.

Mom worked hard for the church, going to Ladies' Aid, being a reluctant officer, consenting after much persuasion to do the program for Circle meetings, baking for a church dinner her famous Lady Baltimore Cake, a project that seemed to take hours of effort as she whipped the egg whites into stiff peaks before folding them into the mixture.

When I went to Concordia College across the Red River in Moorhead, Minnesota, Mom was recruited to be president of the Cobber Mothers, a group that raised money for campus projects. She was also Community Chest captain for a section of Fargo, making calls and recruiting others to make them.

Mother was in demand as a speaker at women's groups. Close to Mother's Day she was always struggling for a fresh talk; programs for mother-daughter banquets were never complete without a quiet message from Mrs. Johnson. As a member of the Fargo Round Table Club, part of the women's club movement in the Thirties, Mom studied and agonized over her annual paper to be delivered to the group. Spread out over the dining room table were pages and pages covered with her tiny "backhand" script, script that made people ask me if she was left handed. One year her topic was medieval street theatre productions, primarily religious in focus. Another year she delved into the French Impressionists. Did she choose these topics for herself, or were they assigned to her? My guess is that she chose them. Here were topics she knew nothing about, and this was a chance to learn.

Right out of college, Mother had become a teacher—German and English, I believe. When I was in college, she somehow connected with Viking Press to review their new fiction. Viking mailed her first editions that she struggled to write about. I say "struggled" because she never thought what she had written was good enough. This unjustified sense of inadequacy was probably the reason she gave up the task, but in the meantime I was proud.

If I must put into just a few words what Mother was, I think the term "self-effacing" is right. So capable, so modest, such a popular speaker, a mother who kept a neat house, and a full cookie jar, but still read us stories at night, and sewed dresses for me and my little sister, but without broadcasting her loving efficiency.

Mom never really knew how remarkable she was in my eyes. Early-onset Alzheimer's took over.

⚏ The Big Test ⚏

When I was twelve or so, I went through the process of learning about the teachings of the conservative church my parents had grown up with. As Scandinavians, they came from the state church of their origins: Lutheranism. They had both been "confirmed," or accepted solemnly into the church in their own hometowns. Although neither Dad nor Mom was particularly "religious" in the sense of quoting the "should"s and "shouldn't"s, they were part of Fargo First Lutheran Church and did as tradition required.

In early adolescence, each of us—Bob, Ruthie and I—spent an hour at church on Saturday mornings during two consecutive academic years, being instructed by our minister in the tenets of the church. In turn, each of us had a copy of *Luther's Small Catechism*, a bound volume about six by six inches. The cover was rough paper, and my copy was "desecrated" by my wandering fingernails as I scratched off letters to make the cover read *her Small Cat*. (Not a defiant response, but an idle one.) In the meantime, I memorized all the questions, their answers, and a Bible verse or two serving as "proof" of their correct interpretation.

In the second spring of classes, we all faced catechization, the oral exam we both anticipated and dreaded. By Fargo standards of the time, our church was big; the center aisle seemed to be at least a block long. In our white dresses or white-shirt-dark-pants costumes, we each stood at the end of a row of pews and awaited our fearsome questioning. Reverend Berge walked the aisle, stopping in front of one of us, then pointing at a trembling adolescent and asking a question: "What is redemption?" A perfectly memorized response wasn't enough to avoid his next question: "What is meant by this?" which we had to answer according to *Luther's Small Catechism*. And if the confirmand was especially unlucky, a third question followed: "What does the Bible say about this?"

I was lucky. My question was one of my favorites. It had a nice easy rhythm and a few polysyllabic words that made memorizing it easy. Reverend Berge stopped before me. (I was tall, so I think I was close to the end of the line, because we had been arranged by height—perhaps for some aesthetic reason.)

"What is God?" asked our schoolmaster.

With certainty, I responded: "God is a spirit who is eternal, almighty, all-knowing, everywhere present, wise, good, merciful, holy, true and just."

Perfect! I was in! Actually, even the mumblers and stumblers were in. After two years, how could anyone be heartlessly excluded? Surely a merciful God said silently, "In!" to us all.

❦ Getting the Giggles ❦

Sometimes Ruthie and I just could not stop. She'd do funny things—like the time she came down to the basement Rec Room on Fifth Street North where we were gathered to watch Dad play pool on his newly installed table. She was barefoot, and the basement floor was cold. While I stood watching the game, she lurched into the room by standing first on the little throw rug in the doorway, then without lifting her feet, walking the rug and her tall self into the room. It was too much, and we fell apart laughing.

She and I thought the Rec Room funny in itself. The carpenters had finished the room with the newest in paneling: knotty pine. Because fashion had not caught up to the notion of knotty pine doors, the imaginative carpenters had dipped their thumbs in brown paint and carefully thumb-printed pine knots at six-inch intervals running in ranks down the length of the door. Never having seen knotholes parading in columns, we couldn't help marveling. And of course, commenting.

We found it ridiculous that, in that big house, Mother thought she needed more storage room, needed our old scrapbooks and Halloween costumes out of the knotty pine closets at the end of the Rec Room. She had plenty of room. What would she put in those closets if we vacated them? We speculated. More ghastly antiques?

When Mom and Dad finally worked themselves out of the Great Depression, Mom could indulge herself by "going antiquing" with the bishop's wife. (Mom's shopping with the bishop's wife was funny, too. She was so stuffy.) Mom had a great time finding odds and ends, some beautiful, like the cherry bedroom set and the walnut secretary, but some weird, like that platform rocker. And the porcelain vase, the one we called the "lady leaning on a pansy." When Ruthie and I admired her new acquisitions, we'd point to the lady leaning on the pansy and say, "You get that." Then the other replied, "No, you do. I get the amethyst vase."

After we had grown up, married, and moved away, Ruthie and I joined one another at the cottage on Pelican Lake only on rare vacations when our dates coincided, because Ruthie's family lived in Geneva, Switzerland—where, I was sure, life was vastly more interesting than in central Ohio. At the cottage, we often spent most of the day at the dining room table, too busy talking to get up until it was time to prepare the next meal. Ruthie's four children, two girls and two boys, carefully planned like mine, joined my four. Sometimes she and I got started laughing and could not stop, gasping at how funny the other one was, and hiding our tears in our napkins. Once, when we were out of control, Jim turned to his cousins and said, "What do you expect? They're sisters."

And then there was the time when Nathan, Ruthie's youngest, looked down at his shirt and asked indignantly, "Who spilled strawberries on my shirt?" Too good to keep. We often tried it for laughs.

A rare career move for Ruthie's family brought them temporarily to Montclair, New Jersey, and the six of us went out to visit them. Ruthie and I could be tourists together in New York City! We'd try not to gawk at the tall buildings, and people skating in the middle of the city—people always skated on flooded vacant lots in Fargo. With wild extravagance we mimicked the sophisticated Easterners. But when we left the City, we had all the acquisitions of awe-struck bumpkins. In the huge New York bus station, as we waited for the Montclair bus, we looked at each other, saw the waving three-foot peacock feathers we'd each bought in Greenwich Village, and started a monumental giggle session that kept us doubled up, leaning on the station walls, and lasted from the Port Authority depot to the car in the Montclair parking lot. We left laugh-puddles on the depot floor.

Rebecca Lukens

✿ Furniture Fondness ✿

Seems a funny topic, but …

First to come to mind is Dad's easy chair in the dining room in North St. Paul where he sat all sprawled out, his long legs extended, his back curved in a slump, away from the padded back. Why he did that, I don't know, but he seemed comfortable. I'd sit on Dad's lap while he patiently read me the funnies from the St. Paul *Pioneer Press*, although of course I didn't get all the humor of his favorite strip, "The Katzenjammer Kids." I could feel him chuckle, so I knew it was funny and I'd try a chuckle. I did see that when Captain Katzenjammer floated on his back, the only thing visible was his face and a round mound of stomach. That was pretty funny.

A big part of the fun was snuggling into Dad's long arms, close up where I could smell his familiar pipe smoke. He liked "Out Our Way," too; it didn't come as a strip but a single square. A gangly adolescent often appeared, with uncombed hair spiky atop his head, shoestrings dragging and too-short pants showing his sagging socks. Dad liked that kid; he said he looked like my brother Bob. Actually, I think he reminded Dad of all of us—Bob, sister Ruthie and sometimes me. I remember one cartoon he cut out and left in the kitchen to remind us that when we cleared the table before washing the dishes, we were not to save and store in the icebox for another meal the most minute scraps. That unkempt kid in the cartoon was saving a dinner plate with three wrinkled green peas on it. Nor did the rest of the dinner dishes and pans all need soaking in the sink. We could finish our job.

When we moved to Fargo, Dad's big armchair held all three of us on Christmas Eve while he read aloud to us "The Other Wise Man," a dull story about the Wise Man who came late, written, as I recall, by Henry Van Dyke who knew little of writing for children. But there we all were. Small sister Ruthie tucked under one arm, I in another, and big brother Bob on the floor, his head resting on Dad's knee. Meanwhile Mom was preparing our traditional dinner of *lefse, krumkakke,* and Swedish meatballs, and Dad's favorite holiday treat: *lutefisk* (cod marinated in lye so it looked gelatinous and nauseating, but Dad loved it.) We used to say that if our noses weren't so close to our mouths, we might like lutefisk; then we'd comment on how lutefisk made the silverware turn black so it couldn't be good for our health. We called Bob a traitor, because he sometimes sided with the parents.

Then we three children grew up, left home, got married and returned with our own kids.

When Dad and Mother bought a cottage at Pelican Lake, there appeared another big easy chair. From its place by the door to the screened porch at the far end of the great room, Dad's chair dominated the whole cottage. Even the huge stone fireplace with its mounted deer head with long antlers (often decorated with fishing caps) couldn't compete for significance with Dad's chair. Once upholstered in blue, it was later cherry-red. The scene changed with the addition of our four kids: Those now being cuddled were two little girls, Janie and Sally, while two boys, bigger and less prone to being cuddled, leaned against the padded chair arms or straddled the footstool while listening to Grandpa Johnson speaking wise words or total nonsense. We revered the footstool that Dad had made in the wood shop in North St. Paul high school, knowing that to salvage four identical legs he had junked five others— unmatched failures. Anyway, that's where Dad sat; sometimes an old green card table was pulled up close while a doting grandchild, often the competitive Sally, lost to him at cribbage or gin rummy. (Her victorious days did come, however.)

Dad's cherry-colored chair was sold with the cottage when Dad died, but we were not bereft, because when he had indulged himself with the first of the new-fangled Barcaloungers for the Fargo house, he sent his old easy chair and its memories to our little house in Fairborn. We had to install the chair in a corner of the attached garage (we couldn't refuse it), along with his big outmoded television set. Whenever I sat in Dad's chair in the garage, I remembered being hugged and read to like the grandchildren. Many years later, when No. 2 daughter set up her home, the many-times reupholstered chair traveled with her to her first Dayton apartment and followed her ever after.

New upholstery could never erase memories.

🔡 My Really, Really Awesome Father 🔡

Dad was awesome, really awesome. He was a handsome six feet three, emanating self-confidence. People used to say to him, "How's the weather up there, A. I.?" By today's standards, he'd be above average and that's all, but to this little girl, he was awesome.

Dad used to read to us in the evening, just as Mother did. Once when I was very small, I cuddled up in his lap and said, "I like you better than Mommy." And he immediately told me that couldn't be true, because they both loved me so much. I think somehow I felt I'd hurt Mother's feelings, and it has often made me aware of how innocently children say such things.

We lived not far from the public school where Dad was principal, then superintendent. On Saturday mornings, he often took me with him while he "monkeyed around" with power tools in the manual training room. I found a picture in my coloring book of a little Dutch girl, traced it, and asked him to make me a plywood Dutch girl. With the power saw he cut it out for me and added a hook or something for me to hang my toothbrush on. I painted it and was proud when he hung it up in the bathroom.

Dad went to law school at night, commuting to St. Paul College of Law. Sometimes my brother Bob, my little sister Ruthie and I were so noisy that he had to study in the car. The first words my sister said—at least that's what I've always heard—were "Mommy, Becky's teasing me." (And I'm sure I was.) But Bob teased me, so the pecking order took over, and I teased her. As we all accused one another and wailed, we must have made a horrendous noise, unsuitable for studying law.

In Fargo, high school was well over a mile from home, maybe two, and I walked some days and rode with him others. He'd drop me off, then go on to his law office. On the way home I occasionally stopped at the office, a little awestruck by the "office lady" who worked in the outer office. When Dad was busy with a client, she'd go in, whisper to him that I was out there, then shut the adjoining door. Once as I sat there, I heard him swear: "Damn" something. The door was closed in no time.

Starting a law practice in the midst of the Depression wasn't easy, and there was very little money for his family. (He borrowed on his life insurance I later heard.) At suppertime, Mom asked what he'd had for lunch, and it was usually a bowl of soup at the Herbst Department Store next door to his office. I just couldn't imagine him at one of those little white cafeteria tables eating a bowl of soup. But somehow I knew it was lack of money that had kept the lunch so minimal.

Dad was an affectionate man, often picking me up to kiss me, or swinging us around. But there was something iron-like in his decisions. I knew he was not to be crossed. When I was little, he didn't hesitate to swat us on the bottom for some infraction of the rules. As an adolescent I once sassed Mom at the dinner table, and Dad sent me to my room. These contrasting behaviors made me both want to please him and to be a little afraid of him.

I went to college across the river at Concordia College, where Dad often took me by car, and I'd walk into Psych 101 smelling of cigar smoke. I was in college, without an extra nickel to my name, but I knew that was where he wanted me to be. When I was little and got my seven cents weekly allowance, I'd put three of them away in my bank for my college education; I'd put two in the Sunday School collection plate, and still I had a big hunk all to myself: Another two pennies of Dad's generosity I could squander. Dad was a loving father, and my children, his grandchildren, loved him.

These memories seem to be those of an adoring child, one who doesn't recognize that old age caught up with Dad. When I went home to visit in Dad's late years—he must have been over 80—May told me how troubled Dad was about the man he had given the second office in his complex to, a man probably in his forties named Garaas. He had thought that Garaas could help his clients when he was out of town, at the lake for a few weeks or on a vacation that May was eager to take, but little by little Dad discovered that Garaas was charging Dad's clients exorbitant fees. And he noted that his law library was disappearing little by little—into Garaas's office. But my tough dad was unable to talk to him, to accuse him.

Armed with May's information, I drew Dad out on how his practice was going, and bit by bit I heard verification of May's story. As he told me that he felt he had made a bad choice letting Garaas into his offices, tears came to his eyes, and I sensed that he felt powerless to do anything about it.

The next day I made an appointment to see Don Hansen, whom I had dated in college and who admired Dad greatly, who perhaps went into law because of that admiration. At Don's office, I met a most sympathetic listener. He had gone to the University of North Dakota Law School and was a classmate of Garaas's. Not only that, but he had drawn Garaas's name for the annual peer evaluation of state bar association members. Don would be glad to do what he could, because, as he said to new young lawyers when they set up shop in Fargo, "A.I. Johnson is the best lawyer around."

Another memory of Dad that needs to be recorded concerns a heavy argument I had with him once when I was home for a visit. It was at the time of the 1964 Democratic Convention, and Republican Dad took off on an anti-President Johnson tirade, insisting that when Johnson's daughter married, she had converted to Catholicism to secure the Catholic vote for her father. I insisted that was an unfair comment, and that she must have made up her own mind on such a serious issue. He was furious with me. "Dad, you brought us up to make up our own minds," I protested, but he was not to be argued with. He shook his cane at me.

❧ Shy to Sure ❧

An email from my daughter-in-law Meg set me thinking. As she was bringing me up-to-date on the progress, or lack of it, in the lives of my three grandchildren, I thought back to my own experiences.

Her Daniel, a senior at St. Lawrence University, had just begun acting in the college plays. Although he's intelligent, clever, funny, athletic, and gregarious, a big handsome young man at six feet four inches, a learning disability has handicapped him, despite his masking behavior, making him feel inadequate. Just this year, he tells his mother, acting has changed him, made him more self-confident, and he's enjoying life more than ever before.

Meg's story about Daniel's change made me think back to my days of shyness in high school. I wasn't musical, couldn't play an instrument or sing, and certainly was no athlete. (Besides, I had a sister who was all these things.) But acting in every play I could changed me.

Probably at my mother's suggestion, I tried out for the Fargo High play, "Anne of Green Gables." And to my amazement, I got the part! Anne was newly orphaned and had to move into the home of her aunt and uncle, her reluctant new guardians. When she arrived, she was uncertain and shy, and even felt unwelcome. But as the play progressed, she became involved in school and in friendships, and was helpful at home. Little by little she changed into a confident young girl.

I remember walking on stage in Act One: Anne in black stockings, black shoes, an ugly plaid dress, hair in pigtails, walking timidly, looking at the floor. Sad, scared and homely, she took just three acts to change into a new person. In Act Three, Anne entered wearing a simple white dress, a different girl, alive with excitement and animated chatter. Before I had a chance to open my mouth, the audience applauded. I was stunned. I could act, could convince an audience of something I really wasn't. I could pretend to be all the things I wanted to be. No one need know about the inside.

What Meg's email also brought to mind was a class in theatre at Denver University, a class I took one summer during my college years. Our lecturer in World Drama spoke of the way in which acting often changes the young actor. As the actor assumes different personalities in different roles, she discovers in herself traits never known before. Pretending to be attractive, or decisive, or submissive, or poised, means the actor must make a change in stage behavior. Voila! "I can *be* this!" and "I *am* that!" A big discovery.

I wrote an email to Meg. "Acting has made a big difference to Daniel. I know just what he means."

🔹 The Day I Dyed My Hair 🔹

Well, I didn't really dye it. The bottle says it isn't dye. For dyeing, you remove the color and start fresh on blank hair, and this is just a rinse that wears off in five shampoos. Dyed hair I have never approved of. Not since I heard Mom whisper about the redhead in church. "It's fraud."

But this is different. Of course I'm a redhead now, and I wasn't before, but this is a rinse. It all began years ago. Our first much-adored child was handsome—I'll skip the superlatives—a boy with red, red hair. We were addicted to him, and as we paraded this wonder before admiring friends and relatives and thrust him upon strangers, I beamed and listened expectantly to their comment: "He has his mother's red hair."

More babies came. Three more in fact, and by the fourth one my hair had long since faded. Strangers looked in wonder. "But where did they get the red hair?" They'd even look at my bald, blonde husband: "Oh, I see, from his father." Finally, I just quit protesting that I used to have red hair. This faded brown peppered with gray wasn't the real me. The real me was a vibrant redhead! But you can't keep that up forever when the response is a doubtful "Oh?"

Years passed, and the Hidden Persuaders were after me. The Clairol ad, "Does she or doesn't she?" got to my husband. He'd stare bug-eyed at the redhead, holding her up to see if she really did, then bringing her close, sure she didn't. I could toss off the fascinating blondes, but the henna-hits made me stare surreptitiously.

A visit to an aunt I hadn't seen since I was twelve did it. She marched across the carpet, peered at me, and raised her arms in the air: "What a pity! The lovely red hair is gone. Just gone!" Drab brown, I admitted, but at least it's honest. "Becky," said my other gray-haired aunts, "you must do something about your hair."

That did it. I bought a bottle. A bottle that proclaimed it was a rinse, not a dye. "Be sure to test a sample of your hair twenty-four hours before using." But once I'd worked myself up to actually take this step toward fakery, waiting twenty-four hours was ridiculous. Just *do* it, I thought.

"For highlights, two minutes." Who wants to settle for highlights? "For subtle tones, five." Why be subtle? I never have been. "For more vibrant color, ten minutes." Vibrant, that's for me. Slowly, trembling, I dabbed the color on. I set the timer for fifteen and smiled confidently at the sudsy mess.

The timer rang, and I was vibrant. I vibrated right off my feet and had to sit down. I was staggeringly piquant, vital, the most alive being I'd ever seen. I re-read the bottle. "Do *not* wash immediately." I stepped into the shower, shampooed and washed and washed with all but Clorox and Comet. But I was still vibrating. Daily shampoos for ten days straight. Then I re-read the bottle. "This rinse lasts for five shampoos, as long as five weeks," it said proudly. Ten shampoos in five days? It might at least have the grace to fade. Just a bit.

Professional hairdressers do not look kindly on do-it-yourself repairs, but she agrred to try. I couldn't say, "Just rinse it out. I'll set it at home." It took a cut, a set, an hour of fussing, a half hour under the dryer, and a parking ticket. But I was improved. People didn't point at me on the street; they just talked behind their hands. Or whispered to one another, "Don't stare at Becky."

One dear soul even said to me, "Tell me, is your hair really that color? Really? Well, you'd never know it was out of a bottle." Bless her. But a recent encounter with the drab-looking wife of my husband's boss troubles me. She complemented me on my red hair, and I did a chatty routine: "Redhead children...those ads...my aunts...took the plunge." And she said, "I know just how you feel. I used to be a blonde, you know."

I shudder to say it, but I let my chin drop and gasped, "A blonde. Really? I'd never guess."

Me! After all I'd been through.

◼ Janie the Blister ◼

Janie was always up to something. She was super-active, a real change from Tom who was somewhat quiet—although it's hard to believe now.

We lived in a big, pleasant colonial house when Janie was a toddler, a house across from the city park on Central Avenue in Fairborn. Since she was a busybody, we used the porch for a playpen. I put up a folding gate across the space leading to the steps, so she had an enlarged play area. Although I have recurring visions of her trying to climb over the porch railings, she did play there for a time.

When sister Sally was born, people stopped to see the new baby, but Janie, at the ripe old age of two-and-a-half, would not be ignored. When the school superintendent and his wife dropped in one evening, the boys went through the living room, I suppose, but probably didn't stop for long. Janie, however, was not to be outdone by some squirmy thing wrapped in a blanket. So she put on a show for us. She went to the kitchen and came back to parade across the living room inside her brother Tom's jacket, sleeves dragging on the floor. We laughed and introduced her to our guests. She disappeared by way of the living room staircase, then returned in Tom's white terry bathrobe, dragging the belt behind her. We noticed her of course, but she didn't linger long. She disappeared up the stairs once again, this time to come down with Jim's shoes in her hand.

At the foot of the stairs, she stuck her feet in the big shoes so she could push them across the carpet. Her final appearance, however, was the most dramatic of all. She came down bare naked, without a stitch on. We noticed.

Always busy, Janie wrote on the wall beside the television with my lipstick. A revealing picture of four stockings hung by the chimney with care shows Janie standing on tiptoe on a stool she'd dragged up close. Her hand was deep in a stocking, one that said "J I M" in sequins. When we played Monopoly on the kitchen table, we tried to keep her from squatting there, a handful of paper money and two hotels in her hand.

The house was totally disrupted when the painters and paperhangers came to paint the kitchen and redo the bedrooms. Furniture was out in the halls, draped with curtains and clothes from empty closets. Meanwhile, Janie found the front door was unlocked. So she took a walk through the porch and down the steps to the sidewalk.

Suddenly I missed her, ran out to look, and there she was, walking across Central Avenue, traffic stopped in both directions. With the help of an adrenalin burst, I caught her up in my arms, ran to the house and locked the door. Careless mother!

But she wasn't in the house for long. The kitchen door leading to the backyard was unlatched, and Janie was off again. Another rush outside, and a hasty return to hook the screen door. The painters, now working in the kitchen, had seen it all. They chuckled and introduced me to a new expression. "She's a blister, ain't she?" I'd never heard anyone called "a pistol," so I agreed that Janie was "a blister." She was that.

When Janie left home, married, and became a mother, she sent Mother's Day cards.

"Mom, remember all the aggravation I used to cause you? I'm almost done."

"I cried and complained and slammed the door, but I never, ever stepped on a crack." (This was sent following my back surgery.)

"Dear Mom, Thank you for not running away from home when I was a teenager."

P.S. Some day the four of you will find all the wonderful sentimental cards you sent, not tied in a ribbon, but saved.

And Tom's immortal thank you card:

"Thanks for all your trips to the principal's office."

Or the one that said, "Looking for Mother's Day cards is impossible. They're all so sentimental."

Then, in Tom's handwriting, a most wonderful sentimental personal message.

Rebecca Lukens

❧ Grandchildren–Bless 'Em ❧

This time it's grandchildren—again. (I wish I'd been close to see and hear Andy, Quinn, Rachel, and Kat.)

Last night was Sally's first night as an adjunct instructor. Since she had to leave for Hamilton by 6:30 for a 7:15 class, I offered to check on Andrea, 11, and Daniel, 13, midway through the evening. I arrived at eight and found Andrea in front of the TV and Daniel sitting at the computer, each with a huge slice of pizza and a glass of milk. (Andrea had even remembered to turn off the oven— something I'd been asked to check.)

"How was the first week of school, Andrea?" I asked.

"Good."

"Tell me about it. Who's in your class?"

"Lots of kids, new friends. And the boy I'm going with is neat."

"Oh? What's his name?"

"I don't know yet, but he's in two of my classes. He sits in the next aisle in Social Studies, and four seats away in Science. I love Science. We're studying latitude and longitude."

I had a sudden feeling I ought to look up "latitude," but that was erased by my curiosity about Andrea's "going with" someone.

Then it all came back to me, the day her Aunt Jane came home from seventh grade at Wilson Junior High to announce that she was going steady. Going steady! I panicked. I'd read about Going Steady, and its dire results. Before the month was out she'd be pregnant! Two weeks later she came home to announce they had broken up. "He wasn't in any of my classes. We only saw each other in the hall, so we broke up." Sounded sensible to me.

Then another memory interrupted: Jim, my firstborn, had come home in the first grade to announce he was going to marry Linda Lovejoy. "I chase her on the playground every day," he said.

Having checked on Andrea, I checked in with big brother Daniel, who was sitting in front of the computer. He rose to hug me. I was pleased that I merited such attention. "How's school, Daniel?"

He shrugged. "OK."

"Good classes?"

"I guess so."

"Girls like your new hairdo?" (The one I call "bed-head.")

"Guess so."

"What's your favorite class?"

"Band." (Predictable.)

"Playing bass clarinet?"

"Yeah."

"First chair?"

"Yeah. I'm the only bass player.

"Good."

A few laconic exchanges later, I gave up, and again he rose to hug me. As I left the family room, maternal instinct took over, and I couldn't resist saying, "The rest of the pizza ought to go in the fridge."

From the living room, came Andrea's voice. "Daniel, put it away in that silver paper stuff."

No answer. On my way to the front door, I asked Andrea, "Think he'll do that?"

"No. He's too spacey. In a few minutes when he forgets, I'll take care of it." This early in life she knows her place. I hope she learns another one.

When our children were young, we planned excursions for every Sunday after church. We'd head for Serpent Mound, Old Man's Cave, or Kentucky horse country, the car packed with a cooler, a map, swimsuits, thermos jug, and picnic basket. Because we didn't want to waste precious time each Sunday thinking long and hard about what we needed, I taped the list inside the cover of the basket, details set down in list form. Soon the four of them had memorized it:

"Cups, paper plates, napkins, silverware, salt, pepper, iced tea, sugar, lemon, apples, cookies, and dinner." Someone standing by the basket might interrupt with, "Ooops, not enough napkins."

This summer Sally and I with Andrea and Daniel took off for Michigan to visit Aunt Jane and Uncle Mike at their lake cottage. One afternoon, as I watched D and A argue about who had dibs on the hammock, a crinkled piece of paper flew from Andrea's pocket off into the grass.

"Hey. That's important," Andrea shrieked. "That's our checklist." Surreptitiously, I picked it up and examined it.

Numbers one through seven were neatly circled, but without details.

Checklist

1 All shoes (No mention of 3 pairs of sneakers, 3 pairs of flip-flops, 3 of sandals, and 2 of water shoes)

2 All clothing (No mention of underwear, socks, T-shirts, jeans, shorts, sweaters)

3 All swimsuits (How many? Including cover-ups?)

4 All sleeping bags (Just 2, really)

5 Camera

6 All bathroom stuff (This could be a problem)

7 (No entry)

Too funny to be helpful. Picnic basket did better.

Last week the Russian Blue named King Tut escaped to go hunting, a first for both of us. Some time later, I learned he wasn't a cozy lap cat. He returned with a baby rabbit hanging from his jaws. He was a predator.

Shocked, I controlled my impulse to rescue the little bundle of fur, which was too paralyzed and panicked to move. But Tut knew what to do. He dropped it. He pushed it around a bit. He encouraged it to run. He caught it. He nudged it. He let it go. He stalked it. He caught it. Then he munched on it. He killed it!

That evening I told Daniel, "Tut had a big day. He caught the tiniest little bundle of fur this morning, a baby rabbit. And he killed it!"

I expected sympathetic sniffles, at least a sad smile.

No. Instead, I heard, "Oh, Nana. That's just the food chain!"

Sophistication! At his age, I knew nothing of a "food chain."

🔹 Cousin Esther and the Piglets 🔹

We didn't often drive out to the Hannaford farm. Furthermore, because of milking schedules, the farm families came to Fargo even more rarely. But Dad still thought of himself as a farmer and therefore had to check on the wheat. And the oats, the barley, and even the flax. (In later years, he thought acres and acres of sunflowers were "interesting," but somehow they weren't quite right for the farm. For one thing, they were so heliotropic that they all faced the same direction—wherever the sun was—and that seemed contrary to the laws of farm plantings. Safflower oil? Never heard of it, although we did finally acknowledge the necessity for soybeans.) On a Sunday afternoon when I was a child too young to protest boredom, we "took a ride," with Dad commenting on how the wheat looked like it might avoid the rust—an airborne scourge of some kind—or how the oats were heading out, or the flax looking clean.

But a couple times a summer, perhaps, we actually drove the ninety miles to Hannaford, ND, to see if there had been hail damage, or if Uncle Carl's or Uncle Louis's farm house had been pitted by hail, showing small pockets of bare wood. Once we got there and saw that the tornado had picked up the garage and turned it around on its foundation. Now the driveway led up to a blank wall, the back of the building.

We had cousins on the farm: for one, Cousin Ernest who was

much older than the others and who later became Speaker of the House in Bismarck. Then there were the twins—Richard, who became a school superintendent in a small North Dakota town, and Roland who later went to Ag school, then back to the farm. And, of course, there was Arthur who some time in his adulthood followed his older brother to the legislature. The saddest news was that Willard, tall and handsome and just out of high school and younger than I, was killed in the Battle of the Bulge where so many very young recruits were killed. (Years later, a cousin sent me a poem the family had kept, a poem I had written while in college, after hearing of Willard's death.)

Once when I was quite young, we arrived at the farm (1000 acres under cultivation plus pastures and fallow fields) to find the sows had produced a slew of piglets. That was a sight to see. Esther, our youngest cousin, who was perhaps five and dressed in her white shoes and Sunday organdy, climbed into the pen and chased the piglets. We laughed to see them scramble out of her way. She was feeling brave, and this was something her city cousins knew nothing about—piglets. When she got back to the house, Uncle Carl and Aunt Emma looked at her, horrified; they scolded and punished her with a good "talking to." Dad told us on the way back to Fargo that Esther had done a very dangerous thing: An angry sow could kill an intruder. I tried to remember if I had encouraged her, or even dared her, to do that dangerous thing. I hoped not.

🔹 Aunt Ruth, Perpetual Giver 🔹

Aunt Stella has had her turn. Today it's Aunt Ruth's story.

Mom's younger sister was a nurse, a single woman who, in my eyes, always wore the most elegant clothes in the world. Like for instance the ocelot coat with the big beaver shawl collar. Who had heard of endangered species? Real Minnesota/North Dakota winter warmth. How I loved that coat. And with it, she wore overshoes with furry tops. She wore sling pumps and fashionable clothes; she was always slim and perfect. Since I was busily biting my fingernails, I thought her slender fingers were beautiful, with shiny pink nails.

In fact, during the time she lived in Fargo and worked at St. Luke's Hospital, she often came over to give my grubby hands a manicure. When, on another visit, my nails were ugly as ever, she brought me a nail kit, a "leather" kit with cuticle remover, polish remover, file, whitener pencil—everything. It was beautiful. But I still bit my nails.

Sometimes Aunt Ruth came over from her apartment close to the hospital to use the Maytag, to do her laundry. And what pretty pink silky things went into the water, then came off the line a few hours later. But best of all honors, I was privileged to iron her linen handkerchiefs! She showed me how. When the iron had warmed enough to make a little sizzle when I put a saliva-tipped forefinger on it, I could start.

"Make the corners sharp… Keep them all square. Spread them out, then fold them in four parts, fancy embroidery on the top corner. Lay them aside in a neat pile."

What an honor—ironing Aunt Ruth's embroidered linen hankies! After Aunt Ruth died, I collected her embroidered or appliquéd handkerchiefs, added them to those my mother had left behind, and fantasized about hand quilting around the embroidery, and immortalizing them all in a spectacular wall hanging. (They are all gathered in a bag still in the closet.)

A couple times, she entrusted me with a task even more important. Those were the days of plucked eyebrows. Aunt Ruth lay trustfully with her head in my lap while I wielded the tweezers and tidied up those narrow arched brows. I was contributing to her beauty. Imagine it!

When Aunt Ruth got a new coat, a sealskin one I think, she turned over to me the ocelot fur. Wonder of wonders. I was in high school and now had a short, fingertip-length treasure—a fur coat made for me through Mom's planning. Enough fur was left to make a neat pillbox hat. As I look back, fur must have seemed inappropriate for a high school girl, but it was free—a hand-me-down. And cheap was important in those times. When I went off to graduate school, times were a bit better for us, and Mom had Gertie Bjordahl, our Norwegian seamstress, make it into a tuxedo coat—with wide bands of ocelot down the front from chin to hem—the pill box hat, and a wonderful, luxurious, exotic, warm muff. Off I went to the snows of Syracuse, New York.

When Aunt Ruth died, both my parents were gone. Brother Bob and Sister Ruth asked me to do the little family talk for the memorial service. I was honored. I told how she had once said of her work as a nursing supervisor, "I never asked anyone else to do a job I wouldn't do myself, no matter how unpleasant." When I stood up there at the front of the church, I saw heads nod. Her old friends among the nurses knew that was true.

I also told of my instructions from Mother when I was a child. "Don't ever tell Aunt Ruth you like something she has or is wearing. She will immediately take it off and give it to you." I knew I shouldn't have, but temptation was sometimes too strong, and I *did* sometimes tell her I loved her blouse, or her broach, or her ring, or her jacket. Mom's instructions I defied, but she was right. The coat off her back long ago, and at her death her most precious strand of pearls.

(Will either of my daughters ever want a necklace of matched pearls?)

🪡 But Not Good Enough for Grandma 🪡

She was really good. I mean, really. Fast. Fancy. No counting. Just clicking. Those four thin metal needles positively flew through the blue and white yarns, and a mitten took shape. A Norwegian mitten with big, perfect snowflakes on the palms and backs wasn't under development for long. It was finished in no time.

I wanted to learn. Well, perhaps I wanted to knit rather than to learn. Learning, I soon found out, was hard. It was knitting that would be fun. Grandma consented to teach, but I never did it right. My stitches were too loose. Or so tight I couldn't get my needle in to make the next stitch. Grandma, who had put aside her own knitting to teach me, found it a frustratingly slow process. On that we agreed.

Casting on, she insisted, was easy. Make a loop over the needle, that's all. And don't let them fall off. *Just _do_ it* seemed to be the major message. All thumbs, I kept dropping the yarn, losing a stitch, picking up a loop that wasn't a stitch and turning it into a stitch. Or dropping a stitch so I made unnecessary buttonholes in the scarf. Nothing was right. Start the row with fifteen stitches, end up with twelve. Start out with ten stitches, end up with seventeen.

"You'll *never* learn," Grandma announced, as she picked up her snowflake mittens once again. She broke my heart. Absolutely. But Grandma didn't know who it was that she was challenging.

After her visit, Grandma left our house in Fargo to return to Pelican Rapids, Minnesota. Now the timing was right for a plea to my mother. An ad in the Fargo *Forum* told of a knitting class for beginners that would meet at Herbst Department Store for an hour on Saturday mornings. First thing Saturday morning I had to walk to church for confirmation class, but it was just a few more blocks down Broadway to Herbst's. I was in.

A bit of a rush, but I made it to class that first Saturday, chose a conservative rusty worsted from the many colorful yarn bins, was guided to the proper needles, chose a simple pattern with a boat neck, and learned another way to cast on. One that avoided the big loops between stitches, matched my stiff fingers' moves to the simple knit two purl two the sweater required, and I was off. Not off and running, but off.

For ten weeks? eight weeks? I met with the class. Between times I struggled along at home. Sometimes there were glitches: The ribs were not K1, P2, but K3, P 1, and it showed. I'd grumble, and stop, then wrap it all up for Saturday's class where that pretty young teacher-clerk could fix it in a jiffy with a pleasant, "There you are. All fixed," and I'd start chewing my tongue and get going again.

When it was almost time for a Thanksgiving visit to Grandma's, I put on speed, put the pressure on, sometimes even stopping in at Herbst's for a quick fix during the week. I was determined to be wearing that sweater when we got to Pelican Rapids. And wear it I did.

Grandma didn't notice, so finally Mother said, "Did you see Becky's sweater? She just finished it, all by herself." Grandma, her pinched face refusing to smile, said, "Yes, I see. There's a mistake in the middle of the front."

Grouchy, I went to the bathroom, took it off, and turned it around. I was glad it had a boat neck. In the back a mistake wouldn't show.

◙ Antiques in the Law Office ◙

When Dad first opened his law office in Fargo in the early Thirties, it was an exciting day for both Mom and Dad. He had met the local attorneys and asked around for a likely spot, finally ending up with a downtown office over a clothing store, a separate office in a suite. Attorney Pete Garborg had just been elected to the North Dakota legislature and wanted someone to take care of his clients when he was away in Bismarck. Pete would share his secretary with Dad. Perfect.

After I started high school several years later, I sometimes rode to school with Dad who opened his office early enough to drop me off for my eight o'clocks. In the late afternoon I occasionally walked to 10 ½ Broadway to catch a ride home. Sometimes I even had to stop to see Gertie Bjordahl who had a tiny cluttered closet of a room on the same level; Gertie, a seamstress Mom trusted more than she trusted her own capable self, spoke Norwegian better than she did English. She often was so pleased with her creations that she exclaimed over my new dress, calling it "chick" or even "woguish." But usually my stops to climb the stairs to Dad's office had to do with hitching a ride home. Once I remember waiting in the outer office with a woman I called "Dad's Office Lady." (She was well beyond being called an "office girl.") I was waiting for Dad to finish his conversation with a client. Suddenly I heard

Dad's voice from the inner office uttering a single forbidden word: "Damn!" The Office Lady promptly rose from her chair, marched to Dad's open door, and said quietly, "Mr. Johnson, your daughter's here!" She then closed the door firmly. The client soon left and Dad invited me in. I sat in the clients' chair across from him at his huge desk while he rustled around in a desk drawer for some hard candy—to distract me no doubt.

As a six year old, I had been far more easily distracted during my first visit to Dad's office. The sparkle of leftovers from Dad's predecessor–two shiny brass spittoons, one for the lawyer and one for the client–caught my eye. My curiosity about their purpose was rewarded by a prompt excuse: "I ought to get rid of those things," Dad said, "but they're kind of interesting to have around."

When years later my son Tom on his travels visited Mom and Dad's house, a home filled with Mom's antiques, he begged Dad for one of the two spittoons which now held potted plants as part of the living room decor.

"Not possible," said Dad.

"Not even the smaller one?"

"Of course not. They're my antiques."

◉ The Fixer Will Fix It ◉

Nothing was ever broken longer than fifteen minutes at our house. Dad would arrive on the scene, look over the problem, and say, "If I had a little binder twine, I could fix that." No binder twine, but he fixed it.

Dad grew up on a farm in North Dakota. When a piece of machinery broke down (horses never did), he and Uncle Carl got to work, exercising their imaginations, rooting around in the machine shed or the barn, and pulling out some oddly-shaped bit of trash that might "do the trick." When work stopped on the farm for a breakdown, it took time and money (time was money) to drive the truck to town to the Hannaford Mercantile. Some "little jigger of a thing" might fix the tractor, or the drag, or the tiller, or the threshing machine. Less work time was lost. No down time on Dad's farm. So, long after Dad left the farm to go to high school and college, he continued to apply his skills. Nothing was ever broken longer than fifteen minutes at our house.

When he visited my family over the years, I'd have a list of odds and ends that needed Dad's attention. The closet door was sticking. The washing machine needed leveling. I needed another shelf in the garage. It was devastating news when he finally, in his eighties, told me, "I don't do that anymore. Call someone."

On the other hand, he didn't mind having someone else fix things. Once, on the day he arrived, he stretched out in my easy chair and asked, "Why is it so cold in here?"

I said, "I'm cold, too. The thermostat is set at the right place, but it just takes the furnace so long to catch up and kick in."

"Well, you need a new thermostat, more responsive than four degrees. Call the furnace man." I did, he paid, and we were warmer by noon.

Dad saved everything that just might come in handy, and one day when my neighbor John at the Knolls was again working on making my bird feeder squirrel- and raccoon-proof, I was reminded of Dad. John said, "I can fix this another way. I've got something in the garage that might do it." A minute later he was back, not with binder twine, but with some oddly-shaped gizmo that must have fallen off some defunct piece of equipment. He then proceeded to fix the bird feeder. But he did say that if he'd fixed it right the first time, it should have stayed fixed. John can fix anything but raccoons.

When I told John about binder twine and its many uses, he replied, "I understand that. When we were hiring at Batelle Research Institute, we paid extra attention to the applicant who had grown up on a farm. They could figure things out. Make things work."

John's treasure trove of things to fix stuff with reminded me of Dad, too. John's daughter Kathy helped Phyllis and John pack for their move to the Knolls. Kathy tells of trying to organize and pack their stuff from the garage. "I'd hold up a six-inch piece of string and say, "Dad, I can't believe you need to save this." Neither John nor Dad could part with anything that might some day come in handy.

It must be Dad's example that made me a do-it-yourselfer. Painting and wallpapering, of course, and I can put a new plug on an electric cord any time, easy. I do admit that I once asked the hardware store man if he sold a new heating element for the toaster; it wasn't making toast any more. The hardware store man said, "I think you should buy a new toaster. They're not very expensive." I did, but I bet Dad could have jiggered it up.

Now my daughter Sally, that's different. She doesn't have to hitch up the horses to fix things, either. One day she made three trips to Ace Hardware, talking to Jeff and Debby about the right replacement piece for her toilet. She took a picture of the inside of the tank, showed it to Jeff, and refused to give up.

True, her final solution was to shut that bathroom door and leave it shut until payday when she could afford a plumber. I understood. I'd bought a new toaster.

🖳 In Praise of Order 🖳

When I was a little girl, I shared a bedroom with my brother Bob. I didn't mind, really, though I probably made a fuss about it periodically.

In North St. Paul, our house, though today it might be called a "flat," was the lower floor of a house owned by Mr. and Mrs. Weinacht who lived upstairs. It was a kitchen, a living room, a big dining room, and two bedrooms, but at first no bathroom. Mom and Dad's bedroom was just off the dining room, hidden by a curtain over a door that I remember as extra wide. Bob and I slept in a room off the living room. At the front of the house I could lie in my bed under the high window and hear the summer sounds of other children playing outside, privileged children whose bedtimes were later than ours. Sounds of neighborhood traffic also proved that not everyone had our early-to-bed rules. Regular hours were part of our lives.

A show flickered on the walls, light from cars going by, light mysteriously dimmed on the ivory walls by sheer curtains that fluttered in the breeze. The window was high above my bed, but I could stand there and peer out. With nothing visible but bits of sky through the branches of the big tree out front, I preferred to lie there in bed watching my private light-show on the bedroom walls.

Early in the morning, before anyone else was awake, I'd dress soundlessly ("Dress when you get up"), hurrying into clothes I'd left on the chair, and tiptoe out to the living room. Just beside the four-by-four floor register that breathed warm air from the coal furnace in the basement was the old green card table. And on it was the inevitable jigsaw puzzle. I knew it would be there. It always was. In total silence, I'd ponder it, and tuck in a few pieces before another voice disturbed me. I loved the moments of solitude, of having the whole house to myself.

Things were always where I expected them to be. My clean clothes in my own drawer. When Dad was up, Mom had breakfast on the table.

Mother didn't work outside the home, as the saying goes. But she worked plenty inside the house. Meals were on time. Order was there, always there. Mom was home when I came home from school—though that's not often possible in today's world. The house was tidy. Breakfast was in the kitchen, dinner in the dining room. We all ate together at the table—at least until Bob's and my lives became complicated by late school activities, debate and news-paper for Bob, plays for me.

When I went off to college, commuting for three and a half years, living in a dorm for one semester, the schedule was still predictable. As I look back, I realize that part of my early security came from this predictability, this knowing my clothes were clean,

ironed, and hanging in my closet. Anything I chose was wearable.
I was lucky. Any meal was ready at the customary time; anything
I brought home was undisturbed—as long as I knew its customary
place. Homework in early years was done at the dining room table,
undisturbed by the Atwater Kent box-and-horn radio. Order was
part of my security.

In 1984, when I attended my Fortieth Reunion at Concordia, a
friend from the dorm who had counted herself lucky to be invited
for dinner at our house, told me she'd loved it. A few days later,
now forty years out of college, she wrote to me of the pleasure
of our orderly house. She spoke of other things, of course, like
carpets, dining room dinners, the family together. I responded very
inappropriately, telling her that during my college years I had been
told that Mom needed notice if I was inviting friends. I didn't
understand why, because meals were always good, simply served
but on time. And I had wanted a more casual atmosphere. Sofa
pillows didn't have to be perfectly plumped, magazines might lie
open, books might be piled here or there, and a throw rug might
even have a turned up corner.

As I look back, I see that I was reacting to my college boyfriend's
house, somewhat untidy but lived-in looking. There Don's mother
might invite anyone around to stay for supper. I remember nothing of the food or the service: All I remember is the spontaneity of
all those friends talking at once, their three son's boyfriends—Bob

among them—and perhaps the girlfriends as well. A quick phone call to my house let me stay. Once Mother said to me, "They've taken you over," and I protested, without really realizing it was the informality and spontaneity I loved. I was not rejecting the order of my home, but rather my mother's need for a formal kind of order.

And yet, when I was a homemaker myself, I adopted some of her ways. Order—but without perfection. Simple meals—open by invitation to any extra child in the house. Dinners held warm in the oven for late singers, football and basketball players. Clothes clean, mended, and in their closets, but inexpensive and adaptable by needle and thread to morning demands from the mini-skirted. The living room and sunroom looking lived-in. Privacy for young guests provided in the air-conditioned sunroom if need be. A Basset Hound doing tricks when called upon. These qualities were different from my own childhood, and were my adaptation.

▣ Seventeenth of May / *Sueten de Mai* ▣

Today is the Seventeenth of May, *Sueten de Mai*—although I don't know how to spell it—or pronounce it. But the day is part of my childhood. Not many of us can claim that.

Dad always had a date for the Sons of Norway picnic, a family date. In fact, he was the Speaker for the Day, and we all had to go. I don't know what he talked about; I think he spoke in Norwegian. Nor do I remember much about the picnic except that I think it was held in Fargo's Oak Grove Park—or perhaps in Island Park.

We ate the contributed food—Norwegian, I imagine—probably ignoring some of the delicacies like blood sausage, pickled herring, *rollepulse*, and *gafflebeiter*, whatever that was. There was probably red cabbage, Norwegian (not Swedish) meatballs, and sliced cucumbers in sour cream. The three of us—Bob, Ruthie and I—hung together, no doubt, and dove into the dessert goodies including *spritz, sandbakkles*, and *fattigman*. We three were aware that it was Norwegian Independence Day but knew little history of Norway—except perhaps that Norway was now independent from Sweden.

The Swedes were an immigrant contingent in Fargo, too, and had their own church, called Elim Lutheran.

❧ Too Busy to Notice ❧

I

We lived in Troy, Michigan, an area of thirty-six square miles, incorporated in order to be called a city, administered by a city manager, and home to several schools. The boys were happy there, taking the bus to school from Troy Meadows, our new development that backed up on acres of woods.

Part of the boys' busyness was their constant fascination with the small wildlife they could find in the fields. Snakes. And lizards. And toads. Primarily. But there were also the woods where they could meet friends from the subdivision and plan the building of their fort. Hours they spent there, so far away they couldn't hear the dinner bell, but were finally summoned home by the disappearance of their buddies who lived close enough to hear *their* mothers call.

Each morning they left for the corner where the subdivision met the highway; there they met the bus. Each morning I made their lunches and packed them in their lunchboxes. At 3:30 they reappeared.

As usual, one morning in mid-fall, they left for the corner bus stop. Or so I thought. At about 4:30 they returned. A bit surprised, I asked, "Late today? What happened?" Giggles. No specific comment.

That evening they played under the street lights with friends, then came home to tell us the Whole Truth. They had taken their lunches off to the woods to work on the fort. *They'd skipped school.*

But—there was no school that day. They'd wasted hooky on a holiday! Too busy having fun to notice.

II

The preceding August, according to the calendar, the day had come to register for kindergarten. Janie's Big Day. We had to go to the school to register. We loaded up the station wagon with three-year-old sister Sally, Janie's kindergarten contemporaries, and their moms. Silence was thick in the car: A big change was about to occur. School. Every day. Except weekends. Having parked the big brown wagon in the school parking lot, each of us mothers took the hand of a grown-up five-year-old and entered the hallowed halls of Big Kids. I held the hands of both Janie and Sally, at least for the moment.

Once in the classroom, mothers guided school enrollees around the room, introducing them to the teacher, then noting every corner of the colorful classroom where the children would be going each weekday come fall. I shepherded shy Janie to the desk and tried not to speak for her as in a tiny, breathy voice she answered the teacher's questions. What fun school would be, the teacher said. Janie wasn't sure about that.

When each child had finished the awesome task of registration, the mothers, children, and I started for the car. Because some of the mystery of school had dissolved, fewer hands needed holding and the car was soon filled with chatter as we took off for Troy Meadows.

Down the highway and partway home, a mother called to me from the back seat. "Where's your Sally?" Horrified and embarrassed, I realized I had forgotten my youngest back in the classroom. I immediately turned the car and headed back. As I ran into the room, I spotted her, intensely absorbed and oblivious to our absence, sitting at a long kindergarten table, her towhead bent over a jigsaw puzzle. I rushed over to her.

"Honey, I forgot you! I'm so sorry. Were you afraid?"

She put one more piece into the puzzle, and reluctantly looked up at me. "Oh, I knew you'd be back."

Rebecca Lukens

❧ Traveling with Ten-Year-Olds ❧
Rachel and Vancouver

How could I get acquainted, really acquainted, with my Grand Rapids granddaughter, Rachel? It was hard to do over weekends, either there or here, and always with one or two parents to spread the attention. Any ideas?

The answer was at hand. The Elderhostel catalog listed Intergenerational Programs; surely there would be something for the two of us. Back in 1990, choices were few. I chose a wilderness week on Vancouver Island, Canada, and proposed it to Rachel and her mother Janie. They jumped at the idea, and we set it up. I flew to Chicago where I met Rachel at the airport—traveling alone at ten! Together we flew to Seattle, then on to Vancouver, a beautiful city in full flower.

Vancouver Island was a big hunk of wilderness with a somewhat small town, and the camp was a true piece of country. For a full week we were outdoor people, living in log cottages, each double room sharing a bath with another grandmother and her grand-daughter, walking over rough terrain to the lodge for our meals, participating in everything offered, walking, eating, exploring.

Cliff climbing was early on the week's agenda. Rachel saw a cliff and was the first to say, "Me. Let me be first." Fearless—she didn't know about risks—although I did. Counselors harnessed her up, clipped on a rope belay, and called out instructions as she scraped for handholds on the sheer rock wall. She reached for and grabbed every tiny bump or outcropping, and laboriously she made it to the top. Now the older boys, chagrined that a ten-year-old girl had already been to the top, piped up their eagerness to try. Although Rachel had been sure she could descend on the rope, repelling down the sheer rock, she looked over the edge to assess the situation and changed her mind. She may have returned by way of walking a trail, but she had done it! Made it to the top! The first one!

During that week Rae canoed in the Pacific, kayaked and flipped over to learn to survive, sailed, camped out overnight, swam, went on an orienteering hike using her compass to move from one spot marked on the map to other marked spots, climbed to a platform in a huge tree in the forest, harnessed up and swung through the trees on a cable attached to another tall tree. Here I watched and thought, "Why not take the challenge?" I harnessed up, climbed the big tree via cross steps nailed there, scrambled onto the platform, got hooked to the wire, gave myself a shove, and swung off into the wilderness. Rachel cheered the only grandmother who had taken the challenge. "Nana, you're really neat!" she called after me.

Reward sufficient for a 67-year-old grandmother. Our scrapbook showed it all.

Son Tom heard about Vancouver Island, and although his Andy was just three, Tom said, "I sure hope you can do this with Andy sometime, Mother." I determined to do just that.

Andy's Turn

Grandchild # 2 turned ten. Ten had been a good age for Andy. He was independent, made friends easily, and was excited by new experiences. So what should we do? This time I found several Intergenerational Elderhostels, clipped descriptions of four, and mailed them off to Andy.

"I always wanted to be an oceanographer, Grandma," he said, "so let's go to Galveston, TX, and learn about bottle-nosed dolphins."

Friend Dave Hirsch knew how much fun Rachel and I had had together, and had an eleven-year-old grandson. He'd go too. We met his Benjamin and my Andy in Houston, and Dave and I rented a car for Galveston. Our quarters were in a dormitory and Dave and Ben our neighbors.

Galveston was the most mosquito-ridden place I've ever seen, but that bothered Andy far less than it did me. The kids had separate sessions from ours at times, and at others we met together to learn all about the ocean, its sea life, and especially dolphins. Each child sat in the front of the classroom, with his name tag on a string around his neck, playing cat's cradle with the string and seeming totally unaware of the grad students who were lecturing. Occasionally there'd be a question, and we elders knew they couldn't possibly answer, absorbed in cat's cradle as they were. They'd flub the answer. Not so. Without looking up from the tangle of strings, they knew the answer every time. Multi-tasking was a cinch when it was interesting.

The swimming pool kept them busy, but the candy machines in the dorm lobby kept Andy even busier. Depression child that I had been, I found the dollars available to the children mind-boggling. I had visions of Andy asking his mom for some spending money, then, without admitting her contribution to his wallet, asking his dad for some spending money. He was rich. Appallingly so.

"What will you spend it on?" was my early question, but when I heard he was buying gifts for Mom and Dad and brother Quinn, I was reassured. However, when we spent an afternoon at a resort with a nature shop and video games, Andy got carried away spending his new-found riches. I recall, for example, a $7 lollipop. I protested, but too late. In the Houston airport about to depart for home, he asked if I'd lend him some money to buy gifts for his mom and dad and little brother. I refused. But not to worry. He had a postcard of a tree frog for his dad, and a candy bar for Quinn.

Quinn's Turn

Then came Quinn, now ten. The mistake was offering Quinn a choice of places to go. At the last minute I threw in the possibility of exploring caves in Kentucky. Quinn, to whom caves were exciting, said, *yes*.

Quinn was a different story from his older brother. Before we left Oxford, he had challenged his Uncle Dave to one-on-one on the basketball court. Quinn came away with an additional $5 and hubris galore. His dad had said he'd match his winnings, so Quinn was a rich man. And a hoarder.

Our housing was in a spacious lodge overlooking the Ohio River, with a big grassy yard and a cement patio where a game of hard-driving dodgeball went on continuously. Although Quinn was the youngest of the group, he threw himself into the game.

Our room was pleasant, with a king-sized bed on the first level and steps up to the loft. Thinking he'd like to live in a loft, I offered him that bed, but before he had opened his duffle bag, he called down to me, "Grandma, there isn't any light switch up here." And I said, "Oh, I'll sleep up there. You can have this huge king size one. How about that?" So I trudged upstairs, while he bumped his bag down the steps from the loft.

Before I had turned the covers back, I heard him. "Grandma, I'm afraid of the dark." So I said, "How about I sleep down there with you in that huge bed?" I went down to join him.

In the night, I hung over the edge, leaving acres of space for him to spread out in. And spread out he did. All over the place. But safe from the monsters who might come out of the dark.

The elderhostel had been described as an adventurous one, with climbing and caving. Caving did not thrill me, but I trailed along with the others, wearing old sneakers because our cave was to be a "wet cave." And it was. We crouched to get through the opening, but it was possible to lean over from the hips and get through. With our flashlights and two guides, we pushed on through the tunnels of rock, watching for outcroppings above and being warned of water deeper than our sneakers below. When we came to a place where crouching to hands and knees was necessary, I chose to sit on a ledge and wait for their return. While kids went ahead with one guide, the other stayed behind with me, trying to entertain me by pointing out blind lizards scurrying across the rocks. When we heard the conversation of the cavers, I relaxed—they had made it back. From an incredibly small opening I hadn't noticed before, the explorers crawled in to join me. I had really missed something: A huge room at the end of the tunnel. I was not envious.

The next big adventure was a man-made "mountain" of timbers and cross-timbers and trapezes and ropes that led up to the heavens.

While sensible adults (over 60, most of us) watched from bleachers, kids took turns trying to reach the top. Each one was in a harness with a belay rope and an attendant to prompt and encourage. Fresh from my aquaerobics class led by enthusiastic Luann, I knew the importance of loud and frequent praise, challenges, instructions: "To the left, just a bit higher. Reach! ... Good job! ... You got it! ... Attaboy, Quinn! ... Just one more grab, and you've made it. Congratulations! All the way to the top!" Quinn and many others had been encouraged to set a reachable goal, and most chose a midpoint. But Quinn made it to the top where he sat triumphantly waving to us and dangling his legs over the final horizontal timber.

Reactions of the grandparents below varied. Some said at the outset, "No way I'll get off these bleachers." Others grimaced and almost had to turn away as they saw the kids' legs tremble with exertion. But one grandpa called himself an ex-Marine, and nothing would stop him from climbing. We watched breathlessly as his legs trembled with the effort, and his fingers slipped from a tenuous hold. We were afraid we might be witnesses to a fatal accident. When he came down by belay, he could not speak for many minutes. When he did, he told us that having had a hip replacement had made it harder than it should have been.

Quinn's pride was boundless. Brother Andy had never done anything like that and we had pictures to prove Quinn's success.

🝊 That Intriguing Woman 🝊

Okay, so I was jealous. I'll admit it.

We four were elderhosteling. She was young. And vivacious and clever. And smart and attractive. And young. A real attention-getter, and holder. She was fascinating. Men hung on every word, young as she was.

Her red hair was a soft strawberry blonde, not a harsh red, but soft and nice in its lines and in its color. Her waist was thickening, I was pleased to see, but she could talk about everything. Her politics were impeccably those of the proper party. She had a job she had created for herself—being the business partner of a group of charitable organizations with headquarters in London. And that meant she could go–and so manufactured a need to go–to London twice a year.

She had visited Parliament!

Once a British member of her "board" had invited her to watch Parliament in action, had introduced her to Mr. Major, the Prime Minister, and had taken her to lunch at the Parliamentary refectory– or whatever it was called. And she'd been assigned a special "tender" who escorted her everywhere, along with the board member ex-Parliament rep.

Furthermore, this redhead could dramatize every bit of the event, the "tender's" manner, his mincing walk, his precise diction, the works. A superb mimic, she stood up to imitate a stiff-necked member of Parliament, with a pompous demeanor and a teacup held with extended pinky.

But that wasn't all. She had another business. She'd answered a newspaper ad for an on-air host, tossed off a flippant résumé, and gotten the job at a St. Louis radio station. Immediately. Before the interview was even over, she was hired to take calls once a week on every topic imaginable, most of them social or political. She surrounded herself with propaganda brought from home, newspapers and magazines, and she fancied herself a popular preacher of the liberal view of issues. (Why hadn't I ever thought of that kind of job? I can ad lib.) She was good. You could see it in her conversational manner and hear it in her words.

Her husband obviously enjoyed her. And appreciated her. He did contradict her, though mildly and thoughtfully. They joined the four of us again for our last dinner at the Napa Valley Elderhostel; she seated herself between her husband and one man, across from the other. She raced on, exhilarated as she talked about our class on Irving Berlin, Cole Porter, and Rogers and Hart, enthralled as she spoke of the class on the French Impressionists. And, throwing herself back against her chair, she demonstrated how bored to senselessness she had been by the fascinating political scientist who explained the politics of the Supreme Court. She was entertaining from wine and salad to dessert and coffee, to the last minute of folding our napkins. (I was silent. I felt old. I said I couldn't hear; my hearing aid was dead.)

As we got up to leave, she hung on her husband's arm and leaned into the other two men, saying, "This was fun. Here's my card. If you find another good Elderhostel, we could meet there. Do let us know."

As we crossed the parking lot, the two enchanted men talked quietly. "Thank heaven that's over. I couldn't stand another meeting with her. Anywhere."

I just said, "She dyes her hair." I, who'd dyed my hair for years, and thought nothing of it. But she was young. Old, but looked young. I couldn't forgive her.

❧ My Love of Beards ❧

Long, long ago, in the city of Fargo, North Dakota, the Fargo
Forum announced that we were having a Centennial Celebration.
Men who thought themselves mature enough to grow a beard were
challenged to grow a beard. Pioneer Days were to come alive— and
Dad began to grow a beard! Exciting.

Without any help from me, that beard became a vigorous reality.
I was away at Syracuse University and had nothing to do with it.
Then one day the mail brought a picture, taken by my sister Ruthie,
the only sibling left at home. What a handsome man he was. Big,
over six feet tall, athletic-looking even at his age. In his business suit
and beard, he looked like a polished Kit Carson or Davie Crockett.
I put the snapshot on my desk and admired it. When the festivities were over in Fargo, Dad shaved it off. Ruthie and I were disappointed, but Mom thought it a good idea.

During my first teaching experience at St. Olaf College in
Minnesota, beards were apparently "in," so students organized a
beard contest. Probably because I was the youngest and newest
faculty member, I was invited to be the judge. (As I look back, my
strongest memory is not of judging beards, but of walking across
the gym floor trying to keep my alligator sling pumps from falling off, leaving me with one leg three inches shorter than the other.

I'd borrowed Ruthie's shoes, and my skinny feet just could not manage them.) I must have made it to the judge's stand because I do remember staging a serious analysis of six student beards.

Years later, son Jim went off to work on Dad's farm in central North Dakota. It was something Dad thought important and Jim thought an adventure. Loaded with paperback books, he left home for a summer month of pitching hay, shocking grain, early, early rising, lunch out of a basket with the crew and in the sunshine—or shade if he could find it. When our aunts, uncles, and cousins–Dad's family of origin–drove out to our Minnesota cottage for a July reunion, Jim came, too. With a thick red beard. His siblings thought he looked great—but different. My firstborn—with a beard!

Jim sported that beard proudly. On our long drive home to Ohio from the lake, we stopped at an ordinary highway restaurant. Strangely, the hostess could not find room for six of us; that, she said, was her reason for putting our bearded family member at a table of casually dressed laborers and semi-truck drivers. When we arrived in Hamilton, Jim took off to see his girlfriend, but when he rang her doorbell, the girl's mother didn't recognize him, didn't invite him in, but left him cooling his heels on the front porch. The next day, Jim reported for high school football practice. The coach took one look and pronounced a new rule: No beards. Mustache? No mustache.

At about this time, our assistant minister at Zion Lutheran Church in Hamilton went off on vacation and returned with a beard. Behind their hands, the congregation took sides in whispers. One elderly woman spoke quietly to me as we walked up the aisle: "I don't like it. Men shouldn't have beards."

I couldn't resist. "It's fine with me. Moses and Jesus had them." She couldn't argue with that.

Rebecca Lukens

⬛ Surviving the Morning Shower ⬛

It's not the shower that's so hard. I can handle hot water and even, sometimes, cold. It's getting out onto the bath mat and having to face that big, shiny, liar of a mirror. When I face the image, I hear myself say, "Who let him/her/that in? We never welcomed *that* at a Knolls Monday-morning coffee. I've never heard its name. I wonder where it calls home? Can it possibly adjust to communal living here?"

As I contemplate the figure in the mirror, I run my hands through my wet hair, making it stand on crooked ends in every direction. Then the right shoulder of the image slumps down and forward, and the arm goes limp across its plump body. Now the figure is all lop-sided, one hand hanging uselessly at thigh height. Suddenly, a remarkable change occurs! The "abominable muscles" of the figure relax. What comfort that must be! What were once called Love Handles move! Now they wrap languidly around what appear once to have been a waist, but are now in the voluptuous shape of a bicycle tire. No, a mountain bike tire, or perhaps a motorcycle.

Next the jaw line shifts. It's clear that a slack jaw is more impressive if it's slack at one side only. The figure raises one eyebrow for a quizzical effect, and lowers the lid halfway on the other eye, thus achieving the impression that "nobody's home." For a final transformation, it tilts the altered head downward to look out from under apelike brows

Now survey this mirrored creature. Estimate its weight. In fact, make an overwhelmingly honest estimate—like 350 lbs. Then, moving quickly lest courage fail, find the bathroom scale—normally hidden on the floor in the linen closet—and drag it out.

Go ahead! Step on it! Yes, the scale. Step on it. Hey! Watch that bouncing, restless arrow! Ahhhh! It settles. Good news: I now know one thing for certain. That *can't* be me in the mirror! I'm a lightweight.

Packing Fig Newtons

My senior year in college, I wanted to live in a dormitory on campus instead of commuting each day, riding to my eight o'clocks with my dad, and entering class smelling of cigar smoke. I needed enough money to stay in the dormitory for at least one semester, and my parents challenged me to earn it. So I spent part of the summer between my junior and senior years packing cookies at the Nabisco Baking Company in Fargo.

In order to be at work on the cookie line by seven a.m., I set my alarm for 5:30, dressed, ate my breakfast, and took off on my bicycle, peddling hard from Eighth Street South to Thirteenth Street North to clock in before seven a.m.

The first day I was assigned to a job assembling laminated cardboard cubic boxes used in the grocery stores to display Nabisco cookies. Beside me was a pile of flat forms waiting to be stapled into boxes. Sitting on a high stool, as instructed, I picked up a flat cardboard form, with both hands held two edges of the box over a right angle-shaped form, thus creating a corner, and tapped the foot pedal. With a thunderous "crack," a huge staple fastened the two edges into a corner. Then I turned the box to place the next two edges over the corner shape, hit the pedal, and fastened a second corner. Thus around the four corners of the box. And then adding that box to the others beside me.

My instructor watched me try the heavy machine, matching corners, hitting the pedal, hearing the "crack" as the heavy staple secured the corner. At every turn of the box, she said sharply, "Watch it! You'll put the staple through your hand. Watch it. You'll put it through your hand." Injuries to a clumsy novice must have loomed before her. Her constant warnings slowed me to a snail's pace, and I was soon taken from the stapler to the cookie line.

Life on the cookie packing line was quite different. Hot cookie sheets, 3 x 3 feet, rattled out of the oven at waist height, the belt moving quickly before me to the next packer on my right. My task was to pick up the bubbling hot cookies in rows 2 and 4, keeping them, as I worked, in a single close, tight group, turning to my left, then placing them in the box on the rack before me, boxes like the ones I'd tried to make. The moving belt rumbled and rattled as cookie sheet after cookie sheet kept coming. Desperate to keep up, I leaned out over the hot sheets to reach cookies in the center of the sheet, scrambling to pick up all the cookies in rows two and four. My fingers raced—so it seemed to me—across the hot greased sheets, while more and more of the cookies in rows two and four were left for workers farther down the rattling line. The other packers had to add the ones I missed to rows they had been assigned to pack. The fastest packers were stationed at the end of the line, their task to pack all cookies missed by packers close to the ovens—like me. The supervisor saw my snail's pace and slowed the conveyor belt a bit. Still, I struggled to do my part of the job, knowing that every cookie I left on the fiercely hot sheet added to the responsibility of someone below me on the line, or else tumbled into a bin of broken bits at the end of the belt. Waste. It was wartime, and I knew about waste!

By noon my fingertips were red and burned.

At 11 a.m., four hours after we had begun our packing, the bell rang for lunch, and the cookie belt rattled to a stop. A kind older woman asked me if I'd like to go to lunch with her, and knowing I hadn't time to ride my bike home, and that it hadn't occurred to me to pack myself a lunch, I thanked her and walked down the block to a small café, one I'd passed many times as I drove down 13th Street but had never seen.

The menu: Creamed dried beef on toast, lunch I knew from home, seemed a good choice. I was starved! But thirty-five cents! I had burned my fingers for a full hour to earn thirty-five cents! I'd worked four hours, and once I'd bought lunch, that left only three hours worth for the dormitory fee. Just over a dollar! Never again. Peanut butter and jelly from home was the only answer.

I'd never liked Fig Newtons, but I came to hate them; their fig filling was bubbling and boiling as it came out of the ovens, the hottest cookies of them all. Sometimes I worked on the cracker table; Saltines came from the cracker oven in three by three foot squares, and my job was to break them into eight-by-eight squares, then into four-by-fours. I packed stacks of hot crackers into Nabisco cracker boxes. Over the weeks, my fingertips either developed calluses or became desensitized.

That summer I learned to put Band-aids on my burned and bleeding fingers, but found the clumsiness slowed me down even more. I worked for two months at Nabisco Bakery, earning enough to pay for a semester in the dorm.

I never ate a single cookie.

The Equal Rights Movement at Our House

When the four children were all home, we had a certain dinner-time routine. First, each of the four had a chance to tell about what happened that day. Sometimes it was a waste of time: Long pauses. "First I hung up my coat.... Then I sat down at my desk.... Then the kid next to me..."

At other times, particularly in the 60s, something significant might have happened. Like the time Tom and his friend Bill were in charge of the high school P.A. system for the opening minutes of the school day. "We decided to play a syncopated version of 'The Star Spangled Banner,'" Tom said, "so we borrowed Pete's José Feliciano recording. It was neat, kind of jazzy. But Mr. Graves came into the studio, jerked the player's arm off the record, and broke the record over his knee! *It wasn't even ours!*"

This announcement, unlike some others, resulted in some group expression of opinion. Actually none of the six of us could see that the sovereignty, or even the reputation, of the U.S. had been damaged by José Feliciano, but the parents present at the table, knowing how important control was at Taft High School—control that forbade individual choice—did think that perhaps it hadn't been "wise" for Tom and Bill to substitute their own choice of patriotic music.

This may not have been the first bit of rebellion, but more followed.

One morning Tom left for school wearing a large sandwich board over his shoulders. He'd spent some time the night before, making two poster board signs, one for his front and one for his back: "MIKE MORGENSTERN DESERVES TO BE IN NATIONAL HONOR SOCIETY" they said. Surprised at this new event, I stopped Tom at the kitchen door, and said foolishly, "But I thought you didn't *like* Mike Morgenstern."

"*That* has nothing to do with it," Tom said. "It's an issue of fairness. He has the grades." When I heard the details, I had to agree.

Events like these were fuel to Tom's egalitarian spirit. He persisted in his fight, acting on principle, inviting his African-American friends to our lily white neighborhood to play basketball in our driveway. Neighbors didn't say anything, which was disapproval enough. He took them home in his brother's old junker and got jeers from that neighborhood, but he'd gotten out of the car to talk with them, and it soon subsided. These were friends, and he'd brook no discrimination. When the principal ruled that there would be no mustaches at Taft High School, Tom was adamant. "A mustache means a lot to the black guys. It shows they're grown up. They can't forbid *that!*" Tom had been Class President for three years and thought foolishly that he might make a difference. He grew a mustache. Rule sustained. He shaved.

◙ Confessions of an Elderly Feminist ◙

In 2001 I was asked to give a lecture for the Institute for Learning in Retirement on a topic of my choice. Several weeks, maybe months, of pondering topics finally brought me to think of the experiences that had made a feminist of me. I agreed to do the lecture/talk, but kept changing the name: *Memoir of an Ancient Feminist. Memories of an Old/Aged/Aging Feminist.* After much grinding of teeth and brain, I settled on describing myself as an Elderly Feminist, because that implied change or transition, not finality like "aged" or "ancient" or "antique." My talk was billed as "Confessions of an Elderly Feminist." Much of my examination begins in my childhood.

In 1964, when Randy took the job of City Manager of Hamilton, I drove to Miami University, which someone had told me was "just down the road." Having taught a freshman composition class at Ohio University–Chillicothe, I timidly thought I might see if I could find a job at Miami. Somehow, I found the Department of English in Upham Hall, and there spoke to Ed Branch who was just finishing his term as chair.

I told him we were moving to Hamilton, then mentioned my experience at OU-Chillicothe, St. Olaf, N.Y. State Teachers College at Albany—a pretty skimpy record, actually. So I added the editorial staff of the Funk and Wagnalls children's encyclopedia, the two (lousy) children's stories I'd published, my pleasure in writing and in editing. He listened.

Actually, I had been in Hamilton to look for a house—in fact, to agree that the Emerson Avenue house was fine. Back in Chillicothe on Monday morning, I got a call from Prof. Branch offering me a job teaching children's literature and freshman comp. I'd be part-time with only six classroom hours. It was perfect. Wife and mother roles would be undisturbed. So began my many teaching years at Miami, 1964 to 1987.

When first I met my new officemate, she referred to a book I had read a year or so earlier, but that had made little impact on me: *The Feminine Mystique* by Betty Friedan. My officemate said that she admired women my age who were returning to professional work/life. I immediately reread *Mystique*, seeing it this time as a personal portrait: Friedan mentioned "the problem that has no name," which I might define as a general restlessness. An educated housewife, restless, isolated by suburbia and child care, looking for challenge, and filling time by having more children. This time I decided the book was about me.

From there I took off, reading, thinking: de Beauvoir's *The Second Sex*; Ellman's *Thinking About Women*; Millett's *Sexual Politics*; *Women in a Sexist Society: Studies in Power and Powerlessness*; *Man's World, Woman's Place*; Heilbrun's *Reinventing Womanhood*; Greer's *The Female Eunuch*, Dowling's *The Cinderella Complex*, and even Mirabelle

Morgan's *The Total Woman* (about meeting one's husband at the door clothed only in Saran Wrap—as a way out of boredom.) And I recalled that popular book circulating among Concordia women intent on becoming ministers' brides: *The Pastor's Helpmate.*

It all made sense. I took it from there, lost my guilt about Randy's worry when I took the Miami teaching job: "Two of us on the tax payroll!" I had a wonderful time teaching. Perhaps you remember dinnertime on Emerson Avenue. When it was my five minutes to tell "what happened today," I was eloquent about teaching freshman comp.

As for that noontime talk, these are some of the memories that seemed relevant. I recalled that when I was a child in North St. Paul, Dad came home from his superintendent's office and told Mom that he had had to fire one of the city's best teachers, a woman who had gotten married over the summer. Public opinion and the school board said that jobs were for men; women belonged at home, and she had to go.

I thought, too, that before she married, Mother was a high school principal. Then I suddenly realized, she couldn't vote. She was extremely self-effacing, a shy but effective volunteer, a reluctant but hard-working community worker, a popular speaker who doubted herself, a woman who sewed for herself and her daughters, kept a full cookie jar and an immaculate home. A woman of smothered ability who had given herself totally to staying home where she belonged, she accepted being a subordinate. When Dad bought a Model T Ford, she wanted to drive, but at her first effort at starting the engine, she cranked it and broke her arm. Dad thought she ought not try it again. She was totally dependent on Dad; although I doubt she resented it, she had no money to call her own, to spend as she wished, certainly not on herself. (Shades of Virginia Woolf's "five pounds and 'A Room of One's Own.'") New in law practice, Dad was asked to be a board member of the North Dakota Savings and Loan, and generously turned over to Mom the $10 he made each month. That may sound like an allowance, but she felt it was a gift. She tucked it away to buy presents for her children.

For Christmas Bob got a bicycle—action, adventure, freedom! My Christmas gift was a picture of a little Dutch girl for the wall of my bedroom. For my birthday two days later, I got a beautiful blonde doll. When several years after that I saw the picture book, *The Girl Who Liked to Climb Trees*, I knew that story. About her doll-gift, she asked, "What shall I do with it?" "Change it." "For what?" "Dress it." "It's already dressed." "Hold it." So she carried it under her arm like a football. How I envied Bob that bicycle that could take him around the block, and even farther.

In the neighborhood we played "wedding," the bride dressed in lace curtains, pulled in the red wagon trailing tin cans for what Mom called a "chivaree." Being the bride was supposed to be an honor, but being pulled in the wagon in a lace curtain got old. So I jumped rope, played jacks and hopscotch, while Bob played mumblety-peg—with a knife—and saw the world on his bike. I heard about Grandma Peterson who had been a Carrie Nation, one of the women who threatened to throw kerosene into the "blind pig," rooms behind a business where men gathered around the potbellied stove to drink in privacy. Grandma was a woman of conviction, shocking, not a violator of a woman's role, but a defender of the family.

As I look back, I realize that in my early adolescence I was reading stories of working women in the popular women's magazines—*Delineator, McCall's, Ladies Home Journal, Good Housekeeping.* However, in those times and in those years, 60% of women entering college dropped out to marry. Educated women stayed home, and had four, five, and six children.

At Concordia, I found classes easy, and when time came for graduation, our class advisor called us together to vote on valedictorian and salutatorian. He wrote in order on the blackboard three names of students with the best accumulated grade point averages: Melva Jean Hegland, four point; Becky Johnson next; and Roy Harrisville last. Then he announced that, traditionally, the valedictorian was a boy (not *man* in those days.) We voted. Roy was top and Melva Jean second. I was not offended, and I doubt she was either. That's the way it was, and it was probably the way I had voted. Two years before at Concordia, Bob was valedictorian, although his fiancée Jean had better grades.

With Mother's encouragement, I applied to graduate school, was admitted to several, then chose the one farthest away from home, the major criterion that sold me on Syracuse. Don Hansen, the boy I had dated in college, came home on leave in 1944 to hear I was going to graduate school. At his home one evening, his mother asked, "But why do you want to go to graduate school? You're only going to cook and sweep." Then she took the huge diamond from her finger, handed it to me, and said, "This could be yours some day." At Syracuse, my major professor stopped in the middle of a lecture and said to us all, "Is that clear to the girl from North Dakota?" Not only was I a girl, but I came from the cultural wastelands.

Then I met Randy and began my total conformity to women's role: babies and housewifery. That first month in Albany, I pointed to a cut of meat in the market showcase, and asked, "What are those?" Filet mignon at two bits apiece. In the grocery, I pointed to Brussels sprouts and asked, "What are those?" "How do you cook this?" was a frequent question. At the end of our first week, my cooking skills had all been displayed, so I emptied the refrigerator, put it all together in a cream sauce I'd learned to make in eighth grade home economics and served it. "We're not *this* poor," was Randy's comment. I learned a little, and we survived. I felt totally inadequate, knowing this was what I was supposed to know and do.

In Albany, I applied for a job at N.Y. State College for Teachers, and as I have told elsewhere in this memoir, was hired because we had no immediate plans for children, then had to quit at the end of the first semester because I was pregnant. During thirty-one years of marriage I made a new home fifteen times, each time throwing myself into making it attractive, keeping a stable sense of "home" for you all. I had no resentment about moving so often, but kept to my role. Only later did I see that women were expected to follow their husband's jobs.

In Indianapolis, I considered applying for a teaching position at Butler University, but fortunately did not even try; we were there only for eight months or so. When we moved to Columbus, I considered applying at Ohio State, until a colleague at Miami reminded me, "Last hired, first fired."

Fortunately, I had been able to teach not only earlier at St. Olaf, but briefly in Albany, then in Chillicothe, and in Hamilton. By commuting several hours a week to Oxford from Indianapolis where Randy and I maintained a home, then from Columbus where we had an apartment, I was able to keep my full-time teaching load. By driving to Oxford Monday night, teaching a twelve-hour class load Tuesday, Wednesday, and Thursday, then driving back Thursday night for four days, I could maintain my wifely duties.

Reading that a happy marriage is two happy people, and feeling responsible for my own happiness therefore, I tried to keep alive mentally. I joined groups. Should China enter the U.N.? How to read an annual report. The ecumenical movement. The Death of God. Situation ethics. Revising the high school curriculum. Theology. Yoga. Books.

Staying young was also an essential part of a woman's role. It meant dyeing my hair, which was rapidly turning gray. Once I encountered a mother and daughter coming toward me and read the little girl's lips: "Which is fake, Mommy, the red hair or the white streak?" Meanwhile, I sewed and knitted for you all, adding a second child, and a third, and a fourth, because as long as I was doing it, why not one more to love?

Magazines were full of projects for women, to keep them busy and happy at their housewife roles. Following instructions, I made a hassock from three big juice cans, covering them with upholstery material. I hooked a rug for the girls' room, made madras shirt after madras shirt, little girl dresses one after another. Using the incentive system, I kept house. "Make the beds, read a chapter. Do the dishes, read a chapter. Write that letter to the folks, read a chapter."

Sister Ruthie, pregnant with her third while I was pregnant with my fourth, came home from Taiwan where she had had servants. She asked, But how do you keep house? I told her you set up a program: Monday wash, Tuesday iron, Wednesday clean the upstairs, etc. I disappeared upstairs, came down five minutes later, dusting my hands and saying, "That was Wednesday." I read aloud to you four in Fairborn, sitting on the front steps of our double while kids from the 101 total gathered to hear the story, too. I tried writing stories, joined a writing group where we critiqued for each other, and learned a lot.

Taking on an overload for the needed money, I taught evening classes at Miami-Hamilton where I often heard women in my classes say, "I'm so lucky my husband lets me do this." And Sally asked me one day, "Mommy, do you still teach at that college?" I was elated. I wasn't shirking my wife/mother role, but had kept my paid job from interfering with my women's role.

All this time, I really hadn't thought much about feminism as it affected me. Then one day I saw a poster in the corridor outside the Zoology department, a diagram of a woman's body cut into meat market segments—prime ribs, spare ribs, shank, butt—and it hit me. In some men's eyes, women were a commodity! At Follett's bookstore, they were selling mugs with the message, "Have you stopped beating your wife?" Several women faculty wrote the manager, telling him to get rid of those mugs or we'd not order our textbooks through Follett's. Teaching children's literature, I realized that catalogs advertised books "For girls" and "For boys." Adventure and excitement were for boys. Passive domesticity was for girls. I wrote to Scholastic Press. I joined a conscience-raising group, one of the thousands around the country organized very loosely around the general topic of women's issues. There I found others who admitted they were poor cooks, didn't like it very much. But more important, I found that many women were eager to break out of their stereotypical roles. I formed close friendships there, though none of us were activists.

Under the leadership of a sociology-gerontology professor, Dr. Mildred Seltzer, a series of classes for community women, classes around women's issues, was organized. I participated, talking at one class about books that define for boys and girls what their lives were to be. In another class, I moderated with two colleagues in English, focusing on novels with strong women, like Kate Chopin's *The Awakening*. Women seemed hungry to find themselves in books. That class went so well that we set up a five- or six-week series using novels by and about women. At that time, the IRS had just set up new rules for publishers, taxing them on their stored inventory. As a result, publishers often destroyed good books that sold only sporadically, even classic drama or Greek philosophy. But since women's lit sold so well, they hung on to those books.

Out of the success of our classes for adult women grew a determination that we had to publish a short story textbook that showed women affirmatively. The three of us set to work finding stories for the anthology to be called *Woman: An Affirmation*, published by D. C. Heath in 1978. It was a reaction to the anthology in common use: *Images of Women in Literature*, which showed women as harridans, whores, goddesses, controlling mothers, nagging wives, all aggressive bitchery or passive nothingness. Our publisher at Heath protested two of our entries: Thomas Hardy's poem, "The Ruined

Maid," the whore who glories in her financial independence, and Doris Lessing's short story, "One Off the Short List," about an unsuccessful seduction. The anthology included poems and stories on childbirth, motherhood, commitment, marriage, and successful aging, folktales with heroic girls, brief memoirs of a few successful women like Lillian Hellman and Maya Angelou, and a play called, "The Chalk Garden." Our anthology never sold well, but became a sort of "when our ship comes in" joke among us.

One day a woman student brought to class a yellowed women's magazine that she'd found in the attic of her new house. It had been published when the WWII soldiers were coming home. The major article preached that women returning from gainful and important work in the WACS or WAVES or the war plants were now to give up their jobs and personal incomes to become docile wives. Written in pen across the magazine page was the comment of an unknown reader: "Nonsense!" My student wouldn't let me keep the magazine. It was too important to her.

Miami joined the many universities offering courses in a program called Women's Studies, a topic some of my male colleagues thought ridiculous. In fact, one of them wrote a letter to the editor of the Oxford *Press,* a letter that drew three faculty responses in support of the new program. Little by little the numbers of classes grew to be a minor, and more. My own favorite was "Women in Contemporary Fiction," a challenge to keep up with because more and more women were not only writing—as they had for centuries under the name of "Anonymous"—but were being published. Good stuff, too. The Women's Studies program was followed by the Women's Center with women's programming.

Somewhere in this period, I walked across campus with a powerful scholar, an African-American woman in our department. At the time I was concerned about college expenses for four children and fearful about income. I confided to her what my salary was. She stood dead still on the sidewalk.

"Well, you have to do something about that!" She gave me helpful advice. I went to the President's Office and, knowing that tax-assisted as Miami is, salary figures were public record, I asked to see the personnel/salary lists. I held the big ledger on my knees in his outer office, as I checked the alphabetical list of all faculty, seeking information about colleagues with comparable experience and education. Since the records showed monthly pay, and some were paid on a nine-month and some on a twelve-month schedule, I had to compute them. Next I wrote a letter to the Chair and to the Dean, noting inequities between my salary and those of comparably experienced and educated men. I asked for an appointment. I showed it all to Randy who said I shouldn't send it; I'd be fired, not rewarded. But it worked. I got a substantial raise.

I knew that girls who wanted to be dorm corridor advisors were not paid—because lots of eager girls were in that labor pool—but boys were paid because they were less interested. And I also heard that three women had taken their case for promotion and salary to the Affirmative Action office, had set up a hearing, and then found the administration merely a paper tiger. They won without the legal hearing. At about this time, there were at one time a thousand such cases in the courts.

Much changed, not only at Miami but all over the country. At first only the feminist extremists were getting publicity, not good publicity. Soon airline stewardesses wanted to be over 30 and married—and won their case. Women owned their own credit cards, took maternity leave and went back to work, and then fathers took paternity leave. Flextime was initiated, child-care centers appeared, income tax deductions were allowed for the expenses of working mothers, and we could say Ms. instead of Mrs. If we chose.

In 1975 the mortgage holders wanted the husband to sign the mortgage papers, even though the wife was making the payments. (I asked about that when we bought the house on Washington Boulevard. The woman banker was startled.) Social Security changed, widows' benefits, homes for abused adults, the right to choose, women as department chairs, shared housework and child-care, women ordained as rabbis and ministers, women organized for political clout, child custody shared.... Television changed from "Ozzie and Harriet" to "The West Wing" with the President's wife a physician.

Time was when the manufacturers of cake mixes were asked, "Why do you ask the housewife to add an egg to the mix? You could include that, too, you know."

"But," said the manufacturer, "women want and need to feel *they* made the cake."

Awareness of the "glass ceiling" seems universal; fathers protest their bright daughters being discriminated against in the work world, Freud's theories about women have been largely dismissed, and women no longer live largely through their children. Many girls and women *want to be like their mothers.*

A few years ago my good friend and colleague went to a new physician, an oncologist. He greeted her with "Hello, Millie. How are you?"

She said, "You may call me Doctor Seltzer. Unless you'd like me to call you Bobby."

Another colleague found in the mail at home a bill for a pap test addressed to Mr. Karl Schilling. Knowing that Karl hadn't had a pap test, Karen addressed the check to the physician's wife.

A lot has happened, most of it good.

❧ Lost at Sea ❧

Once upon a time.....

It'll never happen again.

Eight of us decided to take a Caribbean cruise. A cruise under wind power. Being our own navigators. One of us had been a naval captain. We could handle it. We'd order the lockers filled with good, even gourmet food. We'd do our own galley work. Just leave us a record of what we had in the larder, and we'd go from there. Kate and Dick had the forward cabin. Jane and Arnold had the stern cabin. Barb and Bill had a bunk in the main cabin. And I figured I could sleep on the padded bench in the main cabin, while Scott, a hardy young man of college age, slept topside, better known to me as "on deck."

All went well. Very well. We dropped anchor here and there at various islands in the bright blue sea. We swam off the boat in our life jackets. We snorkeled in the shallow water best known for exotic and varied marine life. We collected stuff. We sampled the goods at island shops. Kate searched for and found Perrier water so she could brush her teeth with dignity. We moored at Tortola. We rowed our dinghy ashore at Virgin Gorda. We admired the homes built high above the beach, and we marveled at how drinking water was imported for wealthy tourists, while natives found any drinking water they could.

We all drank our Stolichnaya cocktails at dusk, while our eager cooks plundered the freezer for our benefit, and we ate extremely well. For some of us the trip was a budget cruncher, but for others it must have been a cinch. Not to worry. Just great fun.

The evening we moored at Virgin Gorda, we heard the enticing music floating across the water, dance music from several bistros/bars/dives close to the water's edge. It sounded good. Inviting. A new experience. Jane couldn't wait. Scott was ready when we were, he said, and stepped into the lifeboat to play impatiently with the oars. Jane invited Arnold to go ashore with us. She coaxed him, she urged him, she pleaded with him, but Arnold was intractable. Blind and deaf to the shore and its activities as an improvement over our quiet berth, he preferred the security of our rocking movement in the swells.

So Jane said, "Let's us go, Becky!" and we dropped into the dinghy. Scott shifted the oars to push us off, and put his back and shoulders to work getting us away. It wasn't far, eager as we were to explore the exotic shore. He pulled the boat up on the strand. We hopped out and were soon among the dancers.

Or Jane was among the dancers. The crowd was a motley assortment. Jane, a good dancer, was much in demand among the older beachcombers. They tapped shoulders, they cut in, and she danced off with one after another. We tried the entertainment at two or three joints, and with the few dollars we'd tucked into our pockets, we bought one or two drinks. No more than that.

I knew it was time to go back to the sailboat where I was sure Arnold worried, while Kate and Dick reassured him, and Barb and Bill chuckled at his anxious predictions. Jane couldn't stop.

"One more dance. Just one more. And one more." Scott, however, detected my concern and readied the boat for us. By now, the surf had risen, and he couldn't head the little dinghy into the shore. Swells kept hitting it broadside. Jane and I, sure we could wade the short distance, attempted to climb over the gunwales just as a much bigger wave hit the little boat. Howling with laughter at our clumsiness in the surf, we sprawled into the dinghy, soaked from bottom to the top of our dripping hair. Scott poled the boat off toward the sailboat. And we fell to the deck, laughing.

A moment later we were greeted by five adults lined up at the sailboat rail, four of them laughing, and the fifth yelling. "Where have you been? Why were you gone so long? Didn't you know we'd worry?" Arnold's anxiety was palpable. Jane and I were laughing, dripping, defending ourselves, and although Arnold wasn't convinced, we were sober. And had had a great time.

How old were we? I can't remember that part. I just know we can't do it again.

🔲 Dear Four of You 🔲

September 1, 2005

Dear Jim, Tom, Janie, Sally,

You perhaps wonder why I've sent you this book, so I'll explain. A few days ago I heard Tom Matthews, author of *Our Father's War*, interviewed on NPR. The writer and his father, a World War II veteran, were estranged, and the writer felt a need to reconnect with his father. He then arranged with his dad to go back to the site of his war service, hoping that the trip might somehow make the two of them understand each other better. The first and last chapters encapsulate that story.

I asked Sally if she knew anything about how her father had lost his hearing, and she responded only that she knew it was a war injury. Probably that is all that the rest of you know.

When first I met Dad at Syracuse, he had recently been mustered out of the army artillery where he'd been for four-and-a-half years. He was using his G.I. Bill money (called by vets the "52/20 Club," $20 a week for 52 weeks) to attend the Maxwell Graduate School of Public Administration, Syracuse University. As we got acquainted, I learned that he had been injured in the Pacific, and had lost hearing in one ear. I learned only a little more. He and four other soldiers had been checking the beach on the island of Grumashima, a tiny island close to Iwo Jima, searching for Japanese soldiers or explosives. They approached an overturned boat on the shore, and as they drew near, there was a huge explosion, set off they found, by Japanese hiding in the nearby cave. Two or three in the party were killed, and the others injured. Dad was picked up by medics—not on a litter, but in a basket. Literally a "basket case," he was flown to a Hawaiian hospital where he stayed for months. Those in his company told him they had not expected ever to see him alive.

When he spoke of the experience, and rarely, he had little to say but did mention that the U.S. Army on his release had offered him a hearing aid, but that he had refused it. He described it as a huge thing with a long black cord leading to a big heavy battery carried in his shirt pocket. (I remember seeing them.) He didn't want to go home that way. Although Dad said everything else was fine, he did have a couple of shrapnel wounds on his face and head.

When he later developed those fierce headaches, I often wondered if they were related to the explosion. He was sent "disability pay" of about fifteen dollars a month. His hearing was a real handicap, and when the ex-mayor of Hamilton was elected to Congress, I suggested that through him he appeal for a larger compensation. I wrote the letter of appeal and he reluctantly signed it. The response was a raise in his monthly check; his compensation rose to about $30.

Details of the story are the best that I recall.

Back to the book: Matthews began interviewing sons of other veterans about their relationships with their veteran fathers. As I read the book, I was interested to learn how similar their cases were. These soldiers had all suffered Chronic Stress Syndrome, behavior unclassified at the time but what in the Forties was called "shell shock." Divorces, rejection of children, depression, alcoholism, and alienation from family were extremely common. Violent outbursts of anger and abusive behavior were also prevalent. Fortunately we all escaped much of that. I have recently read, too, that it is relatively common for a WWII veteran, as he approaches his late years, to talk about his experiences.

Dad did talk a little about his war experiences. As I write this, I think about Arnold Gross, a captain in the Army Medical Corps, whose company opened the gates of Auschwitz to liberate that concentration camp. Only in his last years did he talk of it, although he said very little—and was furious when he heard talk about doubting the Holocaust. I encouraged Arnold to write about the experience, but he said that it had been written by others.

Randy is a quiet man. He endured a great deal. I feel that he couldn't avoid being affected by his experiences, even what little we know of them. I thought you might understand him better once you read *Our Fathers' War*. I think I do.

◙ Making the AP News ◙

For years I had been actively supporting Planned Parenthood. Every child should be a wanted child, neither neglected nor starved, neither abused nor abandoned—but wanted. When my father died, leaving money in trust for the three of us, he also left a sum for the three of us to give to our choice of charitable causes. My sister Ruth, who was working for the World Council of Churches (and was later a Deputy General Secretary of the organization), wrote from Geneva that she'd like a third of the amount to be given to church-related activity in China; Bob and I agreed. Bob proposed that we support the United Negro College Fund, and Ruth and I agreed. My own suggestion was that a third of the amount be given to the building fund of Butler County Planned Parenthood. Bob and Ruth agreed.

As it happened, ours was the first large gift dedicated to the new building in Hamilton. As I met with officers there, I learned more of the history of the local organization. One small clinic in Oxford had burned. It re-opened temporarily in the undercroft of Holy Trinity Episcopal Church where a section was curtained off for physical exams and counseling. At another time, the Methodist Church in Hamilton provided space for the same services. In each case, space was terribly cramped, the project supported by some and criticized by others, its makeshift venues somehow indicating that the cause of family planning was less than creditable. This, of course, was not the case; the generosity of the two churches—coupled with additional local support—said that family planning was a worthy and humane cause.

Privately, I learned something about struggling families in need of help, abused women whose partners abandoned them, then returned just long enough to impregnate them once again. I learned of families living in poverty, families already too large to support, now anxious about an additional mouth to feed. "Incest" was a word I knew but found too shocking to think about. I now knew it was real.

My interest resulted in my being asked to serve on the Butler County Board of Planned Parenthood where I served for two three-year terms, two years as board President. Because of the dedication of a Hamilton citizen who took an option on property for building a clinic, a citizen-contractor who supervised construction without remuneration, and groups of citizens who were trained by a dedicated and trained volunteer in how to ask for money, the building became a reality. The money came, and the building was built.

No one likes to ask for money, but convinced as I was of the need, I did not find it difficult. When I called on the President of Ohio Casualty, for example, I had figures—but no names, of course—on the numbers of company workers who were clinic patients. Earlier the CEO had been afraid of employee anger if it was known the company supported Planned Parenthood. These patient figures changed his mind and resulted in a generous check. Another of my many calls was to a widow whose husband had established a large industry in Hamilton. She gave generously, became a board member, and continued her generosity.

When my board terms expired, I kept track of Planned Parenthood's progress, worried about its incorporation with Cincinnati and Northern Kentucky, concerned lest the Butler County clinic, now a branch of the larger organization, be abandoned. But the enlarged organization was a big success. When protesters burned down the Cincinnati headquarters, caring people responded with overwhelming generosity, and a new, bigger, and more modern Cincinnati clinic resulted.

All over the country Planned Parenthood was castigated for its willingness to present all the options to pregnant women, not only adoption and birth control, but also the option of abortion. While I saw abortion as a last resort, I knew it was the only answer for many desperate women, women too young at thirteen to be mothers, women without adequate financial support, without adequate housing, without adequate health care for their current families, single young women without a home because their parents had literally thrown them out of the house when they became pregnant. Young victims of incest very often had no one to turn to, but were told *they* had seduced a father, brother, uncle.

How would these women manage? How would they get to a clinic for help? What if they had no transportation? No friend or family member to accompany them? I then volunteered to drive these women, to escort them to the nearest abortion clinic, one professionally staffed and sympathetic to the women's frantic search for help.

Many months ago now, I was the escort for my last needy woman, the third, all of them women whose lives would now be easier because they had gotten help, all of them subjected to the taunts and sneers of fanatics lining the sidewalk.

I think back now to the day when, years ago, I was out for an early morning walk while visiting my aunt in her retirement apartment in Minneapolis. I saw a young man picketing a hospital in the next block. Curious, I walked over to ask why he was picketing. "They do abortions in this hospital," he said self-righteously. I felt my pulse race, my blood pressure skyrocket. "How many homeless babies, starved babies, abandoned or abused babies have you adopted?" I asked. "There are none," he said. "They're all being aborted." That was the day I decided that if I had a chance, I'd help in some way.

But to return to my implied title: "Protest and the Associated Press."

Once her little girl Rachel was in school, my daughter Jane volunteered at the Planned Parenthood Clinic of Western Michigan in Grand Rapids, and a few years later took a job there. It was her task to open the clinic in the morning. One early morning, she approached the building and saw broken glass on the ground. Looking up, she noticed that every window in the clinic had been shot out.

Anxious to call the Director and the police, she rushed for the door and found that the knob had been smeared with human feces. When the press arrived they took pictures, but wanted some employee to be in a photograph, either scrubbing the filthy carpet or running the vacuum cleaner to suck up the broken glass. "Any volunteers?" The staff hung back, no doubt afraid of being known as employees of Planned Parenthood. Not a soul stepped forward, no one but Janie. Her picture and name appeared not only in the Grand Rapids *Press*, but across the country on the Associated Press wires. For days she answered malicious phone calls.

I was proud of her. Frightened, but proud.

Rebecca Lukens

🔲 Whipping Up Something 🔲

Ever since I learned how to operate the knee control on Mom's Singer sewing machine, I've loved to whip up things. It might be a blouse, or a simple skirt, or a not-so-simple pair of slacks, but it got whipped up in no time.

Once, in the sixth grade, I suggested to friend Elsie that we make twin slacks sets. She agreed, and I offered to choose the fabric. What a choice! Without any input from Elsie's dad, our minister at First Lutheran, I bought yards and yards of the wildest print, exotic, jungle-like plants all over it. It didn't glow in the dark, but came close to it. Jeans were being sold with a red triangle at the hem, making the legs extra-flared. They were called "Whoopee Pants." Neat! And in that print, too!

We each made our own. Elsie never wore hers. I suddenly felt conspicuous, and soon abandoned mine.

But I kept at it, sewing most of my own clothes. When Jim was born, my first project was a long baptismal gown of white batiste, passed down for that big baptismal event for all four infants. Soon Janie wore tiny homemade dresses; a yard of fabric made one. Sally wore Janie's outgrown clothes, and when I had to let down the hem, they still wore them.

How they hated the old hemline, washed out or drab gray, but now covered by a strip of matching rickrack tape. "No more rickrack, Mommy. No." So I had to make new dresses, and did. A few were mother-daughter ones, but they balked at sister dresses.

The boys presented a new project. Shirts! And boxer shorts. If I had a scrap of fabric, it might produce a tiny pair of shorts for Jim or Tom. One scrap I knew was inappropriate for a Big Boy of three, (pink and white striped chambray), but Jim didn't wear them often, only when an emergency occurred. He called them his "'mergency shorts" and didn't mind their pinkness. Since I heard no protest, I made father-son shirts. The large ones were not hugely successful.

Then the girls learned to sew at Wilson Junior High. In our household, we spoke of "*tomtegubes*," Swedish house elves. More than once, he/she/they visited the sewing room during the school day to take care of a sloppy-looking zipper, or a skimpy seam. I'd hear one of the young seamstresses say, "The *tomtegube*'s been here." No complaints.

🔃 Now I Won't Forget 🔃

For many years I have regretted my failure to record the many unforgettable things my children said when they were small. I used to say to myself, "I'll never forget that!" but I did and I have. Now that I have a chance to record a few of my grandchildren's equally remarkable comments, I'm trying to do that.

March 3

A precious Christmas gift this year was the one from Andrea. It's a framed photograph of me and her taken in the delivery room at McCullough-Hyde Hospital; I'm holding close the newborn Andrea. The little bundle has a red face with wrinkled-up eyes, and is nestled in the soft blanket. Obviously, I am totally blown away by this tiny wonder. (I wish I had a picture of each of the grandchildren at the earliest moment of our meeting.) This March day, when she was here, she saw it on the bookshelf and brought it to me for my customary admiration.

March 4

News today is that brother Daniel is running for Vice President of his seventh grade class. I asked Andrea if he had a campaign slogan, and she said, "No, but he has a t-shirt. Mom helped him print his name, Dan, on the front." Daniel then cut out a big cardboard R, laid it on the shirt above his name, and spray-painted around it. I asked what the "R" had to do with his name or the campaign, and Andrea said she didn't know. But "I told him he should put some words on the back of the shirt that said, "The 'R' is silent."

She thought that was as funny as I did.

March 5

Andrea came over today. We tried solitaire, double solitaire, and cribbage, but we didn't know the rules, so we muddled along, then gave up to play Scrabble. When Sally, Howard, and Daniel came for Andrea, I confessed that she had trounced me. Howard said he had played chess with her the night before, and kept wondering why she was making these moves.

No sense to them that he could see. First thing you know it was "Checkmate!"

October 7

I called over there yesterday and Daniel answered the phone.
"Your voice is getting lower, Daniel," I said. "Did you know that?"
"No, but I do now. Thanks."

November 3

Today Daniel pulled a perfect con job. He called at about 5, asking how I was feeling.

"Fine, Daniel."

"Your back is pretty good today, Nana?"

"Yes, thank you. How kind of you to ask, Daniel."

"Well, I have a school project for tomorrow. I wondered, could you drive me over to Noah's so we can practice?"

"Perhaps I could do that. When do you need to go?"

"Now, right now."

"Where are you? The house on Morning Sun? Okay."

At the Alpha House as they called it, Daniel came out in a short-sleeved t-shirt, no socks, those long shorts with the crotch at knee height.

"Sorry, Daniel. You can't get in the car without a jacket. Why? Because you might have to walk in the cold. See that student with the short-sleeved t-shirt? I wouldn't give him a ride either without a jacket."

Reluctantly, Daniel went into the house for a jacket. Now I saw what he was carrying—a rectangular case and a long canvas something.

"You sure this is for school, Daniel? Looks to me like a clarinet for a jam session."

"Nope. Noah and I are interviewing each other about the book we just read, and this is Howard's interview camera and his tripod."

Okay, so it was a legitimate assignment, but he was pretty pleased with his "your poor back" maneuver. A touch of concern will get you everything.

December 3

Because my Aunt Ruth took such an interest in me and my bitten fingernails, I wondered what I might do for Andrea. This weekend I called her over and tucked into her hand a twenty dollar bill, saying she could get a manicure. Last summer a manicure had been very helpful. So this Saturday, I arranged to pick her up and take her to the Nail Shop. As we waited, I noted that the manicurist said nothing to any of her customers. When Andrea's turn had come and gone, she showed me her bright nails. I asked what the manicurist had talked about, and Andrea said, "She didn't say anything, so I asked her how her day was going …." A twelve year old had to teach her about conversation.

◙ Shoes: Love/Hate ◙

I can't remember the very first ones, because I was going barefoot much of the time when I was little. I loved the grass, its coolness, even its dampness, the way it hid little bumps and tiny stones. We played in the sandbox, among the apple trees in the back yard, and even walked barefoot up the hill to visit the kids at the top. Once we climbed the fence and stole apples from under the trees of the two old ladies (my age now) partway up the block; we must have been wearing shoes, because I remember being very fleet of foot— until the older one of the two called out to us, "You can have apples any time you like. Just ask." A humiliating response to what for me had been truly daredevil action, totally out of character.

My memories of shoes are primarily of oddity. I had very narrow feet and could never wear shoes like my friends'. My lucky friend Gloria had some remarkable T-strap shoes made of a pebbly leather, and I desperately wanted some. (Her father managed a small department store, so she could get anything!) Mom disapproved of those T-straps, thought them cheaply made, but gave in. They must have come only in a wide width, because my major memory of them is of their often falling off. They quickly disintegrated, and proved mother right.

In one shoe store in Fargo I could count on getting shoes to fit: the R & G Bootery. Dad could double park on Broadway, outside the store, and run in to get himself a new pair of black, size 11A "Doctor Shoes." I could buy 7½ , even in 4AAAA or 5AAAAA width. But oh, the styles! Old lady shoes. One pair I had in high school looked like I was wearing spats: gray fabric with two tiny decorative buttons around the neat patent leather instep, and heels. High heels. Maybe even an inch-and-a-half—or three! But despite their perfect fit, they were still old lady shoes.

What I pined for were saddle shoes. All my friends and Gloria, as well as all the girls who weren't my friends, wore saddle shoes. But I wore brown Oxfords, even with a corrective clunky thing on the sole for my narrow feet. I pleaded with Mother for saddle shoes; she finally gave in and with high excitement I went shopping alone. I came home with brown and white *saddle shoes.* Wide width of course. I could get in and out of them without untying them—but *saddle* shoes. My mother took pity. She took me to R &G Bootery and special-ordered some saddle shoes in *my* size. They came, and they fit, and I loved them.

Two years ago the orthopedist suggested that my fierce back pain might be alleviated by my wearing orthotic shoes. They fit. I hate them. They're clunky. I can't get in or out of them unless I untie them. I think back to those special-order saddle shoes, and I yearn as well for the three-inch heels, black suede opera pumps that I loved and wore even when teaching. And when I got dressed up.

Most of all I yearn for my black patent-leather ankle straps. Heels and all.

Orthotics—baugh!

◙ Tender Moments ◙

Sally told me a good one. Sally's dear friend Howard has moved in with the family, and since Daniel and Andrea are in joint custody, living alternate weeks with their dad and mother, they have to adjust to household changes wherever they happen. One day Andrea asked her mother, "Mommy, are you and Howard taking precautions?" (I gulped.) Sally said, "Yes." Andrea replied, "Good. I don't want a baby."

I visited Jim at Thanksgiving. While Meg and I talked in the kitchen, I told her this story. (They have an 11-year-old, Katherine.) Meg's jaw dropped. "Tell Jim," she said. I told Jim. His jaw dropped. Shocked as we were, we had to agree that if Andrea knew all this, she might not become a teenage mother.

▣ Time Slips ▣

Not long ago I noted that the Scripps Gerontology Program was having an area meeting at the Commons, and since no one said I couldn't go, I went to hear about "The Culture of Alzheimer's." For anyone with my family history, that meant, "What's it like for my mother and sister to live as Alzheimer's patients?" Everyone there was either a professional gerontologist or a student in the Miami program, but I could follow some of it fairly well.

The subject of "time slips" means that without relevant memories, each patient will interpret things from a past time, perhaps from childhood, or from an adult experience. The picture shown, for example, might be of a group of young people at a store counter. It evokes a variety of responses, each from the past of some patient.

"They're all buying something."

"Their skirts are awfully short."

"Don't they know to wait in line, not crowd up together?"

"It's cold out. They should dress warmly."

"People don't wear hats."

"There should be some men in that picture."

When listed, these individual comments make a strange group, even irrelevant, but each one represents a time slip, a second from another time.

I recall visiting my mother at home in Fargo during her late days. She came out to the kitchen, saying, "Like my new shoes? Bought them this morning. Took a walk next door to the shoe store. They fit really well. And I found three more pairs." Just then my sister Ruthie walked in and said, " Mom, where'd you find my shoes? I thought they were in my closet."

Decades later I visited Ruthie at her high-rise apartment in Minneapolis. In her sixties, she was planning a luncheon party for our aunt's ninetieth birthday and the table was set with a lovely floral centerpiece. I commented on its beauty. Her response was frightening: "Oh, I picked them this morning. Out by the garage. There were more under the dining room window but I left them. I got these flowers at the deli downstairs." I remarked that I hadn't noticed flowers there, and she said, "Oh, there's a big flower shop there, right in the elevator. But I'm glad I left a few in the back yard for another time."

I understand time slips. Each of them, Mom and sister, was telling her own truth. Just from another time.

❧ Don't Do It ❧

Granddaughter Rachel and her mom were coming to visit. What should we do? Rachel was perhaps eight. Anything Janie and I set up for her would probably be fine, but I wanted to find something she'd not seen before. I asked around.

First there was that settlement of Plain People, in Indiana, perhaps, or Kentucky. Was it called Pleasant Hill or some such? We went. Our room was simple, furnished with a four-poster bed. Floors were of broad boards, and the windows were low, with lace curtains. Rachel hardly noticed. We had dinner at the old-fashioned dining room, but Rachel found nothing astonishing there. Mashed potatoes were mashed potatoes. After dinner we joined others in a big room where the people sang hymns they knew but we didn't. We sat on the porch, then went to bed.

Next day it was on to Old Man's Cave. And here we had something we could all appreciate. One huge cave was almost entirely open; no tight tunnels led there, but we looked up at sheer walls of rock. A small stream ran through the canyon—though it was hardly a canyon: We could see the top. A little boat with two or three passengers floated through.

When the guide warned us that we were about to approach a tunnel, she said she would turn the light on ahead of us, and the last guide behind us would turn it off. "Beware," she said. "Stay with the group. If you get lost, it may be weeks before you are found. If you call out, the sound doesn't carry in the cave. You may not be heard." It sounded scary, scary enough for an eight-year-old. Before we were all out of the tunnel, the light went off. We stood stock still. I put my hand before my eyes, but the blackness was the blackest I had ever seen. I hoped the last guide of our group had clicked the switch to show us how black is black. Surely it wasn't a kid trying to prove himself fearless.

Janie was the impulsive one, not Rachel. As we walked the grounds, we saw tiny openings in the earth, scarcely big enough for a small child to crawl into. While Rae ignored them, Janie was fascinated. I clung to her, not to Rachel. "Remember what the guide said? Two expert spelunkers have been lost, each of them sure an opening was the way to a huge new cave, a big discovery, all their own to claim. They were never found. Remember, Janie? Remember?"

When we returned to our car, Rachel had had a great time. It was Janie who felt cheated. "I'm coming back some time. I'll check out those holes. I could find something."

I shuddered. May she never....

◉ Dear Peggie and Sue ◉

September 23, 2002

Dear Peggy and Sue,

Thank you so much for your thoughtful letter about your mother. I've been thinking about Esther in recent weeks, wondering how she is, wanting to tell her news of me and my family, and to tell her, too, that the 7th edition of my first textbook is just out. She was always so supportive.

I owe much to your mother. I was a young mother of four in 1959 when we moved to Chillicothe, and your mother was the most welcoming, helpful, patient person possible. She greeted me, before we even met, with copies of the Conrad Aiken trilogy about the Chillicothe area and its history. Even before I came, she gave the books to Randy who had arrived earlier than I to begin his job as city manager. I read *The Trees*, *The Fields*, and *The Town* immediately, and was grateful; I now knew a little more about southern Ohio. As you can see, our friendship began before I even met her. From that moment on we shared our love of books, and much, much more.

When I used to stop to see Esther with my two little girls in tow, she made them happy by introducing them to the trunk of dress-up clothes, clothes you two had dressed up in, and that included her homemade Halloween costumes. Janie and Sally loved being a bumblebee and a princess or a scarecrow. Esther made us lunch on the patio, where we marveled at how Bob had planted a tulip tree in the center to shade our lunchtime talk. Sometimes the whole family came, including Jim and Tom, for Bob's steaks on the handsome grill he'd made from local stone. Sometimes Randy and I were dinner guests in the most interesting home we'd ever seen, perched as it was on the cliffside. In the winter, after our gin and Seven-Up, Bob's favorite drink, we had steaks he grilled in the huge stone fireplace. Over dinner we gazed out over the valley below, admiring its serenity and learning its topography. There we discovered the pleasures of birdwatching, admiring Bob's birdfeeder, its weighted innovations that kept away all but his favorite songbirds.

And then there was the farm in the Appalachian woods. I swam in the pond, hiked the hills, checked out the hidden ginseng plants that the locals might dig, and marveled with Bob and Esther at the natural world they both knew so much about.

At that point in my life, I knew nothing about gardening. Esther took me on wildflower walks along the paths that wound down the cliff. She patiently told me over and over again their names that never seemed to stick in my memory. Those I still remember arouse in me a special kind of sentimental recognition. Like toad trillium, false Solomon's seal, and marsh marigolds.

Then there was our little writing group. Esther, who told me of having taught high school journalism to Eric Sevareid in her Wisconsin days, wanted to record the local-color tales Bob told about his patients from the Appalachian hills, tales they told him, and tales he told of them. So a few of us interested in writing got together regularly to read for each other what we had written that week. Rita Puttcamp, who was publishing teen novels, kept us on track. What Esther and I got from Rita was the regularity of producing and an awareness of how things sounded when read aloud—experiences your writers' groups have given you, I'm sure. The support, the regularity, the persistence were good for us all. During those months, I wrote and read for them some children's stories I had worked on while the children were in school. We celebrated together when two of my stories were accepted for publication, and several years later, when my first textbook was published, I traced my interest and my career to those writing sessions.

Last year when Esther sent me the published copy of her memoir, *Other Days*, I loved it—and loaned it to contemporaries. In fact, I was so inspired that I put together some of my own memories I'd written over the years—of growing up in Fargo and later—and bound them for my children under the title *Confessions of an Elderly Feminist*. But my writings cannot compare with those that Esther wrote.

Over those five years in Chillicothe, I often heard of Peg and Sue, what they were doing, their successes and their commitments.

I knew about Peg's traumatic unpledging from her sorority. And about Sue's civil rights march in Washington. Our whole family saw you two married right there in the house we had come to love. In more recent years Esther has sent me news of your children, her grandchildren, copies of Sue's remarkable books, certainly the one reviewed on the front page of the New York *Times Book Review.* We heard about Peg's life as wife of a diplomat, about her project of assembling a library of American literature for the Russian embassy. All together, these created for me a picture of a proud and loving mother of grown children. I could see the effects of Bob and Esther's loving parenting in the lives you were living. Esther's keen interest in first editions of Willa Cather piqued my curiosity, and inspired my own quite different book collecting. When I go to the used book store owned by Oxford friends (who bought what I had to sell before moving to The Knolls), I think of Esther, her love of books, and her love of browsing.

When we moved to Hamilton, I occasionally drove to Chillicothe to see your mom and dad. I'd stay overnight in your downstairs suite. Your dad was always a pleasure to talk to. Not only did Bob take care of all my nearsighted children, but along with your mother, Bob helped me to form my liberal political views, and even made inroads into Randy's more conservative ideas. When Janie was married in a garden wedding, Bob and Esther were there to celebrate—as we had celebrated your weddings years earlier.

Once while living in Hamilton, I even persuaded Esther to go with me by Amtrak to New York where we saw play after play (another of our enthusiasms) in just a few days. I remember her calling hotel room service for wine. When we left, she tucked all the wine glasses into my suitcase, saying, "We paid enough for the wine. We'll just keep the glasses." I have one still. When the train approached Chillicothe on our return, Esther, elated about seeing Bob, dressed so carefully in our private roomette, dabbing on cologne before she hurried to embrace him on the platform. Then, after the move to Brookline, we wrote letters; the letters were followed by my visiting once or twice, even once in her retirement community.

I have long thought that your parents' marriage must have been as compatible as it is possible for a marriage to be. There were differences, of course, but they had such genuine appreciation for one another. That she is now so weak is sad. She had such vitality. How inevitable that even at 99 she would insist upon maintaining her dignity.

Your letter opens such sadness in me. But thank you for your detailed picture of the last days of this remarkable woman. Thank you, too, for this chance to review my wonderful memories of Esther. Love her for me.

~Becky

◙ Dave Hirsch ◙

Dave Hirsch moved from his Oxford condominium to The Knolls of Oxford in June, 2004, and is glad he did. His only regret is that he didn't move earlier, since he had committed himself to the Founding 40 and planned to wait for the second phase. As he says, he "waited for the price to skyrocket," then made his move.

A native of Hamilton, Dave's early childhood was spent in the center of the city where his dad had a shoe repair shop; Dave lived with his younger sister and parents in a one-bedroom flat above the shop. At the death of his mother when Dave was eleven, the family was separated, his sister living in Cincinnati with an uncle's family, and Dave with his dad.

Dave describes his childhood as very happy. Each weekend his father and he visited his sister in Cincinnati, and during the week he was master chef for the two of them. Dave, who now loves to cook, describes his childhood efforts as "steaks and chops and a fire in the oven from dripped grease."

Eternal gratitude Dave extends to a neighbor who offered him $100 so he could enroll at Miami. At the time, "business was bad" and college was questionable. After dormitory living in Swing Hall and Ogden Hall (and hitchhiking to Hamilton to sell shoes on Saturdays), plus a summer spent fulfilling the requirement of

Comparative Anatomy, Dave entered dental school at Ohio State in 1940. The four years in dental school were accompanied by a Saturday continuation of his shoe selling career and waiting tables at the dental fraternity.

Dave enlisted in the army in his senior year of dental school and was commissioned as a First Lieutenant upon graduation. Then he completed his tour of duty in Europe as a dentist in an Engineer Combat Battalion.

Once he had set up an office, Dave married Sylvia Barger, a marriage that lasted 37 years until her death in 1985. Together they have three children: Jeff who lives in Hamilton, Gigi, a physician in Boston, and Mike an attorney in D.C.

—Biography for The Knolls newspaper,"Then and Now."

◆ Confronting "The Patient's Best Friend" ◆

He shoved the first X-ray under the clip on the viewer and, with his back to his audience, muttered something, then ripped the X-ray off the viewer, slapped in another, muttered again. "Surprised your hospital kept this one. Too old."

Seconds later another image of my spine leaped to the viewer, and the muttering resumed: "Something...*mutter, mutter*... arthritis...*mutter*...osteo-something...surgery...useless...fractured vertebra." As he stared at the viewer I became anxious. What did all this *mutter* mean?

Then—"Need new X-ray. Compare." That I understood.

The nurse dropped into my lap a pair of paper shorts, size XXXXL, helped me carefully into the wheelchair, and trundled me off to the imaging center.

While rolling back to the office later, I thought how this experience verified the stereotype—unfair as stereotypes always are—of the surgeon. Without making any effort at personal contact, he and his words made me feel like a specimen, a piece of non-entity spread on a glass slide for analysis under a microscope. Or like the skeleton of a desiccated mouse held by the tail to reveal all my structural machinery. Afraid I'd be dismissed and sent home for another six weeks of physical therapy, I *could not* leave the office until I found some hope. I said, "Do you think an epidural might help?" He said, "Try it."

At home that afternoon, I could no longer be my usual stoic self, but sat down to cry a bit, wondering what relief from excruciating pain I could expect, pain I had circled as "15" on his "scale of one to ten." The words "surgery useless," and "perhaps a pain pill" hung over me. Was that all?

Ten days following the steroid injection in my spine, I was a different patient, someone new for the specialist to deal with. Pain was 50% better, and I'd mulled over my first visit. This morning I dressed carefully for the appointment, to look if possible like a composed woman, who despite her 81 years was someone to be reckoned with. Preliminaries were routine, without eye contact: "Shot help? What percentage?"

Rather than continue this Q and A procedure, I spoke what I had rehearsed during my hour on the expressway. Careful not to lose my temper, or to show either lack of respect or self- control, I said, "Many women, Doctor, feel condescended to by doctors, treated as though they are of little intelligence or importance, dependent always on others for livelihood, information, and emotional support. Older women, perhaps, feel this more strongly than younger ones; some even say they 'feel invisible,' particularly when they are addressed by their first name, as in, 'And how are we today, Becky?'"

(I suppressed an urge to address him as "Bobby.")

"But," I said, "you and I are both intelligent, educated, professional people, and I have some things I'd like you to clarify."

The teenage doctor looked down at me, then slowly sat down. Now, at eye level, we were equals. As I clutched my computer printout about arthritis, osteoporosis, orthotics, surgery, medication or pain treatment, my questions came thick and fast. He answered each one fully and patiently. When I rose to leave the office, I heard with satisfaction his words: "Perhaps we should try a second epidural shot. We'll make an appointment."

Had I changed the world? Probably not. But I felt better.

A few days later I told my story to a contemporary who had seen many, many doctors. "To me, the problem isn't being a woman," he said. "It's being old that gets us this treatment." He may be right.

◉ Clubbing with Books ◉

History of the Club

It's been around for a long time. In fact, this bunch has been asking the same questions of each other and themselves for five years. More? Try seven. More than that? Ask Jean, the archivist. (No names have been changed to protect the guilty.) Every book club should have an archivist. One who keeps track of what they've read together. When they read it. The archivist may, in fact, have opinions of her own about the book, but when asked, may—or may not—choose to read from her little book the opinions of the group. May or may not apologize for her divergent opinion, fake her personal opinion, clean up universal opinion, summarize or try to summarize group opinion, but above all to keep a record of what has been read. And with luck to record the right name for the author of the right book.

The Convening

"Weren't we reading the new Kingsolver book? No?... But we liked her.... *You* liked her. Not *all* of us did.... She preaches.... Does everyone have to like the book, though?... What if we've already read it? Do we still discuss it again?... (*Elinor read it a year ago and wants to know.*) How about a mystery?... No. No mysteries.... How come?... Because two of us don't like mysteries. They're all plot. And two is enough to say No....But some are good.... Well, how about a good memoir?... Memoirs are mere self-indulgence.... But we've really liked some of them. ...How about the Pulitzers? Remember? We were going to read right through the list.... But some are so big. They needed a good editor."

Thus the choice is made. Simply, amiably, and firmly. Subject to change, however.

Placing the order

The next big discussion concerns placing the order at the bookstore. "Who will call in the order? Becky. Let Becky do it. See if she finally has the number right.... It's 9-7900, isn't it?... No. That's the Miami Help Desk.... How about 4-4900?... Noooo. Wrong prefix.... Oh! I've got it now—three. Is it in paperback?... Hang on. Let me ask. Seventeen bucks too expensive?" (*Hand count for number of copies.*) "Elinor, have you room at home to store one more book?... You'll try the library? O.K. Louise, do you plan to buy it in Hamilton?... Make it just four copies, then." *In case Elinor can't find it at King library* "Can we order an additional copy by next week? Does the store have trouble returning an extra copy?... No? ... We can add another? No problem." *(As with one voice, everyone reminds everyone else of what they all know.)* "Pick it up on Tuesday. 20% discount."

The Convening

Brown bags and books in hand, the group meets at noon at another place that became necessary during the intervening month: Root canals, knee replacements, etc., may intervene. Salutations and happy greetings, followed by various settling in comments: "Who wants tea? Coffee? Iced tea with lemon? No lemon? Oooooh.... Guess what! I forgot my lunch. No, don't get me anything. I don't need anything. I don't deserve it.... Here. Jean, have half my tuna sandwich.... Some of my potato chips? They're baked, not fried.... Fruit, anyone want another apple? I packed two.... v8! Not again, Louise. You're disgustingly healthy already.... Carrots! The inevitable carrots. You must be trying to make up for last month's unbalanced diet.... Please pass the grapes." *(In order to simplify the appalling responsibilities of the hostess, grapes have become fruit du jour for every meeting.)*

The Discussion

The discussion wanders, reminding Edith of a trip she took, Elinor of a character she read about elsewhere, Jean of something we read just a month ago, Louise of a better choice that might have been made, and Becky of a book she used in class and that they should have chosen instead.

The Farewells

"Bye, you all.... Bye, see you in a month.... Great meeting. Good luck.... *Hey!* Don't go! We haven't decided on the next book. Or the intended day. Or whose house.... See you. Call me. I can have it.... Me, too.... You know my number."

◧ Andrea's Goodbye ◧

This summer Sally's companion had a fatal heart attack. Since the two of them had been living together, making plans for the future, it was heartbreaking for us all. For the memorial service in Peffer Park, Andrea asked Sally if she could talk about Howard, too. And she did. Holding a yellow tablet—which she waved rather than referred to—she stood to greet the many adults. "I miss Howard…. He was generous. Always buying gifts. Tomorrow I'll be eleven, and this t-shirt was his present, but he never saw me in it." She looked down at the t-shirt inscription: 'Chicks Rule.'

"Howard was fun. Howard liked to do family things. He was a packrat, a stuff collector. Howard liked music and had two guitars. He loved chocolate. And coffee. Howard was a news junkie, and his house had lots of newspapers."

When the adults had all finished their sharing of Howard memories, I spoke to Andrea's Uncle Jim.

"What did you think of Andrea's little speech?"

"It was great. She had a thesis, and each paragraph supported it. Then she finished with a summary. And she meant it."

A friend who knows Andrea says her name should be changed to "That Andrea."

❧ Greece with a Tall Blonde ❧

Sal had just finished her MBA, I was finishing a research semester in Luxembourg, and it was time for rewards. For both of us. Would she join me for a flight to Spain? Or a cruise through the Greek Islands? Which one? Her choice.

She chose, it was Greece, and we were off.

We flew to Athens from Brussels. The *Herald Tribune* had been full of Belgian controversy about a national language. Feelings were high for French? For Flemish? As we signed the guest register at the Brussels hotel, a cannon went off. I jumped. "Is the country at war over a national language?" "No," said the desk clerk. "That was the cannon that opens the European soccer tournament." We were ready for anything.

Athens is pretty old. We knew that. But that was no excuse for a hotel room that smelled like a sour cotton floor mop. We— I—protested. The surprised desk clerk had no idea how a sour floor mop might smell (I knew; I'd lived in a New York walk-up), but gave us another room—another flight farther up. It smelled like a sour floor mop. We took it.

The streets of Athens were fascinating. Surely "fast food" had originated in Athens. Every second shop was a 6 x 6 foot place open to the street that sold gyros. (We later heard, "A Greek gets a hundred dollars together—he opens a shop.") We walked and stared and window-shopped and consulted our Fodor's *Guide*, finally settling for consultation at an open-air restaurant with numbers of round metal tables fronting the square. Since all were occupied, we asked a dark-haired young man if we might join him. We had no expectation of conversation, but he was very talkative and spoke excellent English. He'd lived in Los Angeles for several years, had had his own hair transplanting business while living there. But because his parents were growing old, he wanted to be back in Athens with his family. And there in Athens he had opened a shop. Was business good? Yes. "The Greek men are proud of their hair; they dread going bald. Business is very good." And so was conversation.

As we talked at length with Dominic—I admit, I did most of the talking—he asked if we would like him to show us something of Athens, and Sal and I caught each other's eye before we said yes. He suggested we meet him and a friend at a popular restaurant for "real Greek food."

That evening Sally and I—me a gray-haired grandmother and she a five-foot-eight blonde—met Dominic and his friend at the busy restaurant, where customers were seated at long tables. He ordered a typical dinner for us, then turned to his friend and, until dinner was over, spoke Greek with him. Sally and I, until dinner was over, spoke English with each other. He politely asked how we had liked the Greek food, and we left together.

Dominic dropped us off at our hotel, but not before inviting us to his family home the following evening. It was his "name day," and he, with every other Greek named Dominic ("four out of five of us are named Dominic") would be celebrating with their families. *Sounds interesting*, Sal and I said to ourselves, *so let's go*.

Dominic picked us up at the hotel, stopped for a few minutes to show us his attractive apartment, then took us on over to his parents' apartment. There, infinite numbers of Greek family members, all of them with shining black hair, all shorter than we, were speaking Greek at high volume and amazing speed. Sally and I were introduced to Mama and then were seated side by side on the sofa—so we could speak English to each other. No one else spoke to us.

This was Greek family life: Mothers, sisters, female cousins, female grandchildren of all ages swarmed about—serving course after course of gorgeous Greek delicacies to the many males: fathers, brothers, male cousins, male grandchildren of all ages. No wonder we'd seen no women on the streets of Athens. They were all at home cooking, making babies, and serving their men. Dominic was lost in the mob, and Sally and I spoke English with each other. Then, with his usual gallantry, Dominic offered to take us back to the hotel. We thanked his mother for the party, and left.

But now, a slight change occurred. As we pulled to the curb at the hotel, he turned to me—the mother—and asked my permission to take my daughter to a Greek nightclub—if she would like to go. He promised to bring Sally back safely at an agreed-upon hour. I gulped, thought a minute, considered her age—23—and her experience, and thought, "O-o-o-kay." A nice young businessman who had told us about his business, his past, his brief marriage to a California woman, who had taken us to his home and introduced us to his parents. Sal, though quiet, seemed agreeable, and I said O.K. if she wants to go. They dropped me off and drove away.

Up in my room, I was stricken.

What had I done! My daughter, alone with a man in Athens, one of the biggest cities in the world. He was the soul of courtesy, but we didn't really know him. I lay down on the bed and tried to forget about it: "She's not a teenager. She's been away from home, at the huge University of Maryland, at music school in Vienna, traveling in Europe. She's not dumb; she can recognize danger." But I couldn't sleep. I just waited for the door to open.

Punctually, at the appointed time, Sally stood in the doorway. I was relieved. Shaking her head, she stood there, hands on hips: "Do you know what he asked me? He asked me to stay in Athens and marry him. Was that why he showed us his apartment? So I'd appreciate his standard of living? I thought all along he was interested in *you*. You're the one who did most of the talking, Mom."

Dominic, in mentioning his brief U.S. marriage, had said "I like American women; they're so wonderfully independent. My wife came to Athens with me, but didn't want to stay, so she left."

Sal didn't stay, either.

◙ At Eighty-Three ◙

April 20, 2006

Dear children, all four,

Today I'm in the mood to comment on myself at 83.

Life is good. I never expected it to be so filled with satisfaction on so many fronts. "Count your blessings" advice, given to those who are discouraged or depressed, never seemed good advice to me. Nor, I suspect, did such advice do much for other advisees. But that's not why I write.

Today I count many pleasures in my life.

At 83, I'm healthy. I can hear—with the help of technology. I can see—after two cataract surgeries. Blood pressure and cholesterol are under control. After spinal surgery, I walk better than I did a year ago. At 83, I have adequate funds, and some long-term care insurance.

At 83, I take great pleasure in talking books with four reader-friends. My efforts to learn the game of bridge show some improvement. I admit that if the four of us spent more time really pondering the rules, we'd be better players. Such pondering, however, would cut into the 94% of our time spent laughing.

At 83, I live in a perfect environment for anyone my age. The house is the right size; I'm surrounded by things I've collected and cherish. The needs of my yard for mulching and trimming are taken care of for me, and my housekeeping amounts to an occasional dusting. The touch of a button calls Resident Services, and any problem is solved.

At 83, I still have theatre tickets—two series in fact—with people I've long known and loved. The Knolls van takes me to the Cincinnati Symphony with others when I wish. The Miami Artist Series and other Oxford events are within reach by car. And I can still drive.

At 83, my friends are close by, some within a block, and some a half-mile away. One of my four wonderful children lives close by so that I can see her and her two delightful children. My other three, two sons and a daughter, check in with me periodically.

At 83, I still have opportunities to teach. Thirty adult women just concluded a six-week term of ILR classes (Miami's Institute for Learning in Retirement), in which we have discussed literature "By and About Women." My brain still responds with an adrenalin rush when I stand before a classroom, and surprisingly, words don't often fail me.

At 83, the 8th edition of my first book is out. *A Critical Handbook of Children's Literature* first hit the market in 1976, the year I turned 54. The royalties have made my life easier.

At 83, I have just been elected by my fellow residents to the Board of The Knolls of Oxford. It's a new experience for me to be working with a decision-making group of Oxford citizens.

At 83, as George Balanchine once said, "I like Now." Looking back is a pleasure for me because my sense of humor still keeps life in perspective. I'm unafraid of what's ahead, and refuse to anticipate a despairing end. I love you all, and all's well.

Besides, optimists live longer.

Rebecca Lukens

◙ Betty Friedan: I Beat You to It ◙

I hadn't thought of it, but in a way, it's true. When my fourth child was still in diapers, we lived in Fairborn, Ohio, next to Wright-Patterson Air Force Base. Each home had several children; in fact, in our block of doubles, I counted 101 children. Like other mothers, I was confined to my little house, restless, eager to revisit the outside world, and—perhaps—not as content to be restricted as some seemed to be. One day, I came up with an idea. Why not suggest a class for housebound mothers?

Before my marriage, I had taught speech. Why not offer a class that required explaining and illustrating a familiar process. I'd offer the class for free. Fairborn High had evening classes for adults, and when I saw that the mayor's wife had registered for my class, I had misgivings. But it wasn't long before ten women listened to each other describe making bread, or sewing on a button the way a tailor does. There was no pressure, and the classroom was as much fun as I remembered.

A few years later, still homebound in Troy, Michigan, but with our fourth child now a toddler, the nearby City of Royal Oak, Michigan, called for adult ed classes. My proposals for "Speech for Clubwomen" (I knew a little about basic Robert's Rules) as well as "The Art of Conversation" (I'd just read a book about it) were soon listed in the city paper. I'd do it for free. Free classes, however, were apparently worthless. No one came. Next term, each class now offered for $10, boasted ten women. Giving a committee report, chairing a meeting, and basic parliamentary procedure were useful skills. Once again—with a "job" that required thinking and planning way beyond three meals a day, keeping up with the laundry, and changing the beds on Fridays—I had a ball. Again a neighbor baby-sat for me, and I "watched" her children on Fridays while she shopped.

Next, we lived in Chillicothe, Ohio, and the youngest was in nursery school. Now I could substitute in public school. Once I "taught " French, wondering whatever happened to my college skills. The day I was assigned a geography class, I did learn about the kinds of soils found in the U.S., including *chernozem* (Russian for "black soil"), the rich muck that grew wheat in North Dakota. Students locked me out of the study hall when I left the room to post the attendance report in the hall. Then Jim came home from high school, embarrassed, to scold me for walking in the hall carrying my books at my side "like a man." He told me, "This is how a girl carries her books," and showed me, cradling them in his crooked elbow. Subbing wasn't for me.

Next, Ohio University opened a branch campus in Chillicothe; the city was delighted, and so was I. I applied to teach a night class in freshman comp (I'd taught it in Albany that one semester before I was fired for becoming pregnant) and loved it, even paper grading.

One evening a week I made a tuna casserole for the family to warm up in the oven, and I was off and running.

Randy took a job in Hamilton, Ohio, and I was left behind to sell the house—something I had done before. One weekend, I found care for the kids, and drove to Hamilton. Over lunch with a councilman, I said, "I understand there's a college around here." He launched into a description of what sounded like the Star of State Schools, and gave me directions for a visit. Once there, I found the English Department, spoke of my minimal experience, the children's encyclopedia job in New York City (brief though it had been) and mentioned having tried my hand at writing stories for children. Two had been published in a children's magazine, a poor one but the only one being published for that age group. Two days later, my Chillicothe phone rang, and I was offered a part-time job at Miami University.

When we moved to Hamilton, the homebound part of my mother-job had been phased out. I told no one of my job at Miami because I was afraid of what the neighbors would think: "She abandoned her children." And Randy was worried that there'd be repercussions about both of us on the tax payroll. However, had neighbors heard my youngest ask me a question at the dinner table, I'd have been cleared of that accusation. She asked me seriously, "Are you still teaching at that college?" I had not upset the four of them, apparently! They didn't need me to be at home while they were in school. At the dinner table, each family member had five minutes to tell "what happened today." As the boys later recalled, my five were filled with the excitement of teaching 18-year-olds to write complete sentences. I hadn't neglected the children. I had made their lives more interesting, and mine as well.

The day I showed up for that first class at Miami, my new office mate, Marilyn Throne, heard my tale, looked me over and said, "*The Feminine Mystique* personified." At the library I found a copy, and in it discovered the common restlessness of educated house-wives. She called it "the problem that has no name."

Betty Friedan, I beat you to it. I'd lived it.

🔳 Hamilton's "Fresh Air Fund" 🔳

It was summer, 1969. From the Lutheran pulpit Reverend Kampfe announced a new program sponsored by Prince of Peace Lutheran Church in urban Cincinnati. To give inner city kids a chance to see another life, a family might invite a child to visit for a week or two. We thought about it, Randy and I particularly. The kids weren't particularly interested, but they were into their own things: Jim working construction, Tom anticipating college, Janie with a summer job at the nearby Dairy Queen, and only thirteen-year-old Sally free floating. It was Mom's idea: what difference would it make in *their* lives?

"We" signed up. In the mail came several pages of blue ditto information: *Act natural. Be aware that, out of pride, he may be inaccurate as he describes his home, his food, his family. These children come from a part of the city where privacy and freedom from noise and dirt do not exist. They may have some money to spend—immediately—on candy, gum, or pop, perhaps their major source of nutrition at home. Don't worry about it. Until she trusts you, she may try to hoard anything you give her. He may not be used to your foods, and hesitant to try them. Encourage, but don't insist. Don't leave money around; these children may rarely see either bills or change and could be terribly tempted. If they say "Yes, sir," or "No, ma'am," accept it or do as you wish.*

It is the hope of the program that host family and child will learn about other people and other lives, another way of living, and both feel less fear or animosity. Perhaps the connection once established will continue over later months or years. Be aware, however, that this experience may not be easy for any of you.

Days later we drove the station wagon to Cincinnati to meet Debby Greenwood, age eight, whose father worked at a tavern (or perhaps was an habitué), and her mother at a nearly hospital. Debby was described by the social worker as very cooperative and friendly; although she did not attend Sunday school, she did go to some of the group programs.

It wasn't easy to find Debby's house, two blocks from the church and behind a store at 1524 Race Street. Half a dozen kids were sitting on a six-inch step along the strip of sidewalk between the stores. Her house faced that narrow sidewalk, and, though we'd been told a bit about what to expect, the apartment was still a surprise. Greeted by a woman in her twenties, I walked immediately into a bedroom with three double beds neatly made. There was barely room to open the door, but the TV was on. Beyond the front room, I could glimpse another room, one that seemed to be the eat-in kitchen. Debby's sister Alice, with her year-old child, was in charge. Another suburban woman had already come to pick up two cousins, her guests this summer.

From somewhere came a pudgy eight-and-a-half year old, smiling broadly and wearing a spotless blue shirt and turquoise shorts. We said our goodbyes, and Debby, still smiling, staggered down the walk with her suitcase, calling her goodbyes to her assembled friends. I offered to help her with her heavy load, hefted it, then asked if she had rocks in it, it was so heavy. She looked surprised, but soon caught my smile, and denied packing rocks.

As we drove through her neighborhood, she called attention to familiar spots, all within about six blocks that were apparently her world. She had lived in several places, gone to school across the street, swum in the pool there—when her mother let her. "The big teenagers try to drown you everyday. They'd had a car once, but someone "made my Dad run up a tree and wreck it." She'd been to Detroit and when she goes some place again, she doesn't know if it will be Detroit or Africa. "You ever been to Africa?" She watched the passing urban landscape from the car window, and unaware of distances, noted that there were no cows, as she had expected.

The route from Cincinnati to Hamilton had once been farmland, perhaps including cows, but by 1969 it was a commercial strip. When we drove up to 697 Emerson Avenue, Hamilton, Debbie said, "So this is a farm." I explained apologetically that we just grew grass and flowers, but that we'd see a farm another day.

We'd been warned that pets might frighten Debbie. When I alerted her about meeting our dog, she was quiet, then told me that a bad dog lived near her house, and he bit kids. But Jason, our

Basset Hound, welcomed her, wagging Debbie off her feet. Late that first evening, about to take a walk with Jason, I asked if would she like to come. She looked alarmed, but timidly said she'd like to go. The instant the door closed behind us, her eyes grew big and she clung to my arm, anxiously weighing it down with her eagerness for reassurance that everything would be all right—in the dark. She had never been out in the dark before, not even to her sister's house around the corner.

"I'll sure be glad when we get to the street light," she said. "Where are all the stores?" "Do you know any people in these houses?" "What's that, what's that?" at every bush.

With great delight, I spotted a rabbit in the shadows, and hoping Jason wouldn't dislocate my shoulder when he caught the scent, I whispered, "Be quiet. There's a bunny rabbit. We don't want to scare it away, and if we're quiet we can watch it sitting so still."

"A bunny rabbit. I don't want no bunny rabbits. I hope Jason scares it away, so it won't bite me." We spotted another dog. "No, not two dogs. No. I never want *two* dogs." Seeing neighbors sitting on their front porch in the evening air, Debby saw activity and lights and said, "Oh, *there's* the store."

We walk in the grass, another experience; shoes off, we feel the soft green. Not Debby. She kicks off her shoes at the driveway and jumps rope in bare feet; for the grass, she needs shoes and socks. "It prickles my legs." A daytime walk in the neighborhood woods was filled with new adventure—and fear. Tiny, harmless beetles and gnats frighten her. "We don't have no bugs, 'cept skeetos, and lightning bugs and water bugs and roaches. Not no other bugs."

Unpacking Debby's suitcase was another discovery. She had brought quite a few things, all clean and ironed but dingy and gray. When I exclaimed at how many clothes she had brought, her reply saddened me. "We thought Dorothy and I would be going to the same place, so we put some of her things in with mine." But two pristine new hand towels and two "face rags" and a bar of soap were her very own. Two little pant-dresses (perhaps one was Dorothy's?) were new and stiff, bought for the occasion, and I thought of the sacrifice her mother had made, buying them with her minimum wage job. Since she left for the hospital at 6:30 each morning, she must have stopped to buy them on her way home.

My own youngest was thirteen, and though I've had four who at one time or another had been eight years old, I'd forgotten the laundry situation. While I stopped at the laundry to pick up dress shirts, Debby slipped into a store and bought a chocolate Fudgesicle. Her spotless clothes, put on for the trip to Krogers, were full of drips. Trying to be inconspicuous about it, I slipped some of her clothes into the washer, the first time with bleach, and the second with bluing. Debbie had described her back porch as having some "iron chairs," a table, and a washing machine. How was it loaded, I asked myself. With a pail? A hose?

Who wouldn't settle for rubbing things out one by one in the tub or the basin? Perhaps once in a while a Laundromat for sheets?

As we had been told, money was for candy. The close presence of stores in the inner city constantly tempted anyone with their wares: 15 cents for a big pickle, a dime for an ice cream cone, and a nickel for gum. Debbie had brought with her 61 cents, and was eager to find a store. We did manage to put off that lavish expenditure until we needed to go to a store. Treating Debbie like my own, I suggested she might like to earn a little. The first job was to vacuum the floor in the tiled Rec Room. A corner here, a corner there, and a little in the middle, no better, nor worse than most eight-year-olds. Putting newspapers into big brown sacks, a new experience, was worth another dime; she did it diligently.

Food was something new, too. "At home, when my mama has a Saturday and Sunday off, we have grits and sausage, or bacon and rice, but when I fix my own breakfast before school I always have toast." Kool-aid was Debbie's name for orange juice—down the hatch. No matter. She could name long lists of food they had at home, from pinto beans to ham, collard greens to round steak (ground steak?) for "gramma who can't have no other kind of meat and no salt." Perhaps she was reciting the variety of the school lunchroom, but she knew them all. As instructed, we all ate the usual Lukens foods, and as we'd been told, she cleaned her plate each time, as she said—"lest when she wanted it, someone else might have been there first." We put limits on ice cream in the freezer. For the first time in her life, Debbie made cookies one Saturday morning with Janie's help.

Debbie loves to swim. She just can't swim enough with those "bad teenagers trying to drown us kids" in the free pool in the schoolyard across the street. As I heard this during our trip from Cincinnati to Hamilton, I wondered how we could manage a swim. New London Hills Swim Club didn't sound right. Although there were many socially conscious people there, there might be others eager to have us evicted. More important, what about comments the other children might make—some spoiled and some merely tactless?

The city pool nearby might be the answer. I went to see the pool manager, a coach who knew my sons, and asked his advice.

"I'm afraid they'd make it miserable for her. In the past three years, we were once invaded by a bunch of trouble-making boys. Other than that time, they just don't come."

"What about the other pools? Are any of them racially mixed?"

"Well, yes, in theory, but not in practice. In one pool we had some little black children, but they were mistreated and never came back. The only possibility is the Booker T. Washington Center pool."

But we hadn't taken Debbie from the inner city to be insulted, or to be the victim of stares, to be uncomfortable in any way, or to find herself taken by her white hosts to an all-black pool. So we drove the twenty miles to beautiful Hueston Woods State Park where she had a marvelous time, splashing with other children in the new swimsuit Janie and Sally had rounded up for her. Our picnic was sandwiches—something new. She refused the fresh fruit.

Debbie seemed not to miss the activity of the streets. I was surprised. To this outsider, it had looked exciting, all the exchanges back and forth, routine question-answer chants and calls. Debbie talks about what they do at home, and has written two short notes home, on the diagonal, across the sheets of wild teen-age stationary. Here she seems completely happy to jump rope and wander around and talk.

Sister Alice, chief baby-sitter, "has a penny bank for her baby and no one knows where it is, 'cept me and Dorothy and Alice and my mother." The list excluded the obvious. "My dad doesn't know where it is, and I'm glad.... Cuz he'd spend it on wine." Careful provision is made that someone is at home when children are. Even the fifteen minutes between mother's return from work and school letting out is covered by Sister Alice or Grandma. I didn't understand Debbie's emphatic statement that all her letter writing is for each member of the family, and "last of all, my Dad."

Alice does the ironing and seems to live there much of the time. She is "three ways safe," Debbie said. She puts a butcher knife under the lock and over the lock and locks the door to her own house around the corner.

Debbie did finally see the country, the farm. On our way out of town, she spotted a small herd of cows huddled near the bridge. We hadn't expected her to have seen a cow, but we weren't ready for her delight at seeing a bird. "Right out there in the yard!"

◉ Wearing a Kerry Pin in Canada ◉

When I dressed on Thursday morning for our bus trip to the Stratford Shakespeare Festival, I wasn't sure if I should wear the pin. But going to "another country" as a U.S. citizen was a bit off-putting. With our currently abysmal international popularity as we "go it alone" in the Middle East, I wanted Canadian citizens to know that I disapproved of "our" policy—and I put "our" in quotation marks.

Wearing the pin, however, was not a mistake. Eleanore Vail had mentioned that the Irish she had met on her visit there were very cordial, even seeming to approve of her Kerry badge. The graduate student daughter of a friend had been in Paris this summer, and when she sat in a restaurant waiting to be served, or even to be noticed, she discovered that she was not welcome: "We do not serve Americans," she was told. As a news junkie, I was aware that we have few allies in the Iraq War, although the coalition of tiny islands had joined the U.S. in its attack.

But wearing the button was not a mistake. The man sitting ahead of me on the bus turned to say to me, "Too bad, but he hasn't a chance." Bad news, but we talked further.

In the Indigena Shop, which featured crafts made in all parts of Canada, the attractive young clerk engaged me in conversation. "It's interesting," she said, "how many Americans seem to want us to know that they do not favor American policy." She smiled and seemed pleased with my button. The waitress in the Canadian lunch shop noted the button, and said, "So many American customers seem to want us Canadians to know they aren't *all* in favor of the Iraq War."

While sitting on the sidewalk bench—and Stratford has lovely sidewalk benches—I was joined by a man from Michigan in his forties. "Glad to see that button." He went on to express his sadness about our domestic programs, including education and medical care, programs that are lacking funding because of the enormous costs of war. His wife was shopping, but he'd rather sit for a while, he said, to express his concerns. "I wish my friends would think more about this election. It's important."

Two young women waved to me as they crossed the street, calling over their shoulders, "We'll have to get to Florida in time to vote for him, but we'll be there." Two college students eating lunch in the park spoke up, too. "I'm working to register voters at home in Alabama. I hope it makes a difference."

Wearing the button was not a mistake.

❖ Jim Packs His Bag ❖

We lived in a double house in Fairborn, part of a block of them, close to the Wright-Patterson Air Base; the little town was filled with young families. Both military and civilian families had "baby boom" children; one day I counted 101 children in our block, almost all of them of elementary school age or younger.

We had no television yet, and apparently didn't feel the need for it, but our home was the site of terrible deprivation for Jim. Every evening, just before supper as I recall, he trotted his five-year-old self to the other front door in the building, the Sangsters' house on the other side of the living room wall. And there he followed the adventures of Davy Crockett and the Lone Ranger—programs absolutely essential to his happiness.

One day, following the usual "Why don't *we* have a TV?" complaint, he disappeared into his bedroom, emerged with a brown paper bag, quietly opened the front door, and, as he had threatened to do, he ran away from home.

Suppertime came, and I knew where to look for the runaway—next door, on the other side of the living room wall, sitting on the floor before the TV, with his brown paper bag.

If you're running away from home, no toothbrush needed, but you'd better pack your pajamas.

Rebecca Lukens

☙ The Boys ☙

When Tom's birth was imminent, I asked Jim whether he wanted a baby sister or a baby brother. (Stupid question but every parent asks it.) Jim's reply was "I want a baby clown." He told Tom much later that that was what he got.

When Jim and Tom were little, I used to cut their hair with an electric clipper; a plastic attachment kept all the hair one height for a buzz cut. While they sat there, the boys amused themselves by eating Cheerios one by one. One morning, out on the back porch, I was cutting Jim's hair—and the attachment fell off. Before I knew it, I had clipped his hair down to a bare bit of scalp, a silver dollar size of white! As usual, Jim wanted to know how his haircut looked in the back. Somehow—I just couldn't put my hands on the hand-held mirror. Lost, I guess.

◼ Marine Research: Ten-Year-Olds ◼

On August 9, 2003, two ten-year-old cousins and their 80- year-old Nana took off to become marine biologists. Katherine Rebecca Lukens and Andrea Jane Christman had only met for a week over a year before, but now they were friends in adventure. An intergenerational Elderhostel was our destination.

Wallops Island turned out not to be an island after all, and the limousine that brought the three of us to row house number 61 was not a limo but a big taxi. It was late, the campus was dark, and small, 25 watt bulbs dimly lit the entrances, but the key fit the lock. We walked in. There, on the left, was a dark bedroom with twin beds. "Monsters live there," shuddered Kat and Andrea. Nana steered them to the room at the end of the hall, lighter and bigger. "Let's carry the extra bed from the monster room into our room, then Nana can sleep with us, " someone said, and the process began.

Shoving the mattress off one bed, turning over the heavy iron base, and grunting, struggling, pushing, lifting, they got the bed down the hall to the back bedroom and back together. Now there were three beds in one slightly larger room. Followed quickly by one backpack, two suitcases, two stuffed animals. And very soon by suitcases overflowing with clothes and raincoats and even two blankies. Then came Nana's suitcase.

Bedded down in the lamp-lit room, Kat and Andrea asked Nana, "Aren't you afraid of monsters, Nana?" "You mean, you're not afraid of the dark, either?" Nana admitted having been afraid of the dark once upon a time—because her brother jumped out at her some-times—but admitted that she "learned not to be afraid" of the dark when she had to reassure her own children, Jim, Sally, Jane and Tom that "there was nothing to be afraid of." As for monsters, Nana said she'd never seen one. "Aren't you afraid of anything?" asked Andrea. "Well, yes, I am afraid of falling," Nana said.

The next morning, Nana decided that the monsters' room looked inviting in the daylight, private and roomy; she moved into it.

For a week, everyone was a marine researcher. All of us— six girls, three boys, and seven grandparents—learned about the shore and the ocean. We walked the wetlands in the steamy mist—Nana in a green garbage bag for a raincoat—and heard about the shore-birds, the egrets and pelicans, saw an abandoned oyster market, carefully walked the old dock to pull up a bucket of water spec-imens, identified algae, eel grass and kelp, and heard under our feet the crunch of broken oyster shells that served as beach. We saw how the vegetation changed from low-growing plants with shallow roots in the sand to taller and taller bushes and even small trees as the soil became more firm away from the water. And the two of them decorated their faces with black muck from the bottom.

Back at the lab, Kat and Andrea and their friend Teal made slides from the water that had been saved, dripping a single drop on a glass slide, covering it with a tiny clear square, tapping bubbles out with a finger, and carrying it carefully to the microscopes set up on the long lab tables. Beside each scope were two books, line drawings of plankton. Teal squealed excitedly over her slide: "They're wiggling! I can see them!" Immediately the others were at her shoulder to see. Another squeal. "I can't find any!" "Mine don't move!" "I got a bunch!"

They searched the books to name their specimens, drew pictures to show Ashlie, Gwen and Mandy, the instructors. Hovering over each scholar was a helpful adult.

Another day they explored the shore of Assateague, the wildlife preserve where, each year, wild ponies swim across the narrow straits to Chincoteague to be sold for pets. This day researchers all played Beach Bingo. Armed with plastic bags and a paper marked in pictured squares, each one showing something to be found on the beach, they went beach combing. Kat and Andrea found, dusted off, and identified each piece, even filling the free square for Sand in the center of the page, as well as something called "detritus," better known as trash.

When someone won (with lots of help from a grandma) interest waned, but the bags were full of treasures to take home and identify.

Andrea washed her finds under the hose, put a towel on her bed, and laid them all out according to kind: lots of kinds of clam shells, whelk, oyster, and even some with weird names like gooey ducks that Nana could never remember, although Andrea and Kat and Teal could. Then the six girls and three boys all played in the waves, and later climbed dripping wet onto the bus at departure time.

One evening the lab was the scene of a demonstration of equipment needed for the voyage of exploration on the Marine Science Consortium trawler. Mandy showed us all how to set up the clear cylinder to be dropped into the ocean by a line marked in feet. An intricate system of tight rubber covers at top and bottom had to be secured so that when the cylinder reached the right depth, a "messenger" of lead would drop and close the tube, trapping water at a certain depth. Andrea and Kat had to hook it all up, and next day on the boat, they managed perfectly.

Next Kat and Andrea learned about using an alcohol thermometer to test this water's temperature, and drops of chemicals to test density and salinity. At the back of the boat—the stern, actually—the girls had to know how to attach the trawler net, to use the compass to find tidal direction, and to measure by knots on a rope how fast the water was moving.

But the boat! That was the exciting thing! Life preservers, many instructions about boat behavior, research stations for each crew of three, descriptions of tasks—all new stuff.

When Captain Tim stopped the trawler, and the trawl net was reeled in, the deck was alive with excitement: "A loggerhead turtle!" screamed Mandy. "Look! Big one, fifteen inches across! An endangered species! Look hard and fast. We have to throw it back right away." (That night Mandy called her mother—so excited she alarmed her, but delighted her, too—with news that to a marine scientist is great.)

That wasn't all the net held. Jellyfish. Clams. A big stingray that later waved its flat body gracefully in the lab aquarium. Lots of other stuff, too, got dumped into the big bucket to return to the lab.

One evening a guest marine scientist came to tell everyone about horseshoe crabs which were around millions of years before the dinosaurs. Under the table, scientist Jan had an open cardboard box with some stick-like thing waving around in the air above the box. When Andrea and Kat and the others had heard all the mysteries of the crabs' lives, Jan asked who would like to touch one. Andrea was fastest on her feet and soon held it up, a huge high crown of a shell ten inches across and one stiff antenna moving in circles to sense directions and surfaces. Warily, Kat touched the crab's stomach, and Andrea gave Teal a turn at holding the monster.

Another afternoon in the lab was demanding. Long lab tables held microscopes, glass dishes with specimens of all kinds, from exotic blue crabs to needle-like ocean worms, and beside each specimen was a printed sign: "Phylum—." Now, with the help of the textbooks,

Kat and Andrea and Teal had to identify the specimen by family, genus, and class. The lab was quiet. One young scientist sought advice from another. They shared differences of opinion. "But this is wrong for that.... It curls too much for one of those.... Isn't that a tiny tentacle there?" One by one, with patient help from Mandy and Gwen, the list of identified items on the blackboard grew.

Watching the children jump into the waves at the beach on another day gave grandparents on the shore some anxious moments. Nana sat on a low sand dune and each time a wave broke, she counted to six. Over and over to six. I never counted to six so many times in my life, but the head of every young marine scientist showed up every time. The boys didn't join the girls but did their own jumping in other places.

The last evening was a surprise party. The long lab tables were covered with newspapers. Twenty wooden mallets held them down. Ashlie carried into the lab a square tub of hot water, opened it, and brought out a bowl of spiced shrimp and steamed clams. Then! Blue crabs ready for pounding and cracking and twisting claws and tasting and marveling and getting gooey to the elbows. What a feast.

Before we could get our diplomas, Teal and Kat and Andrea and all the others had to tell one thing they'd learned (like "I learned that black sand from the bottom has no oxygen and brown sand has, and that means something about the kinds of things that grow there.") And introduced grandparents who had to tell two things they'd learned. We all did.

We all had a wonderful time. And next day we went home reluctantly.

—For Kat's and Andrea's diaries, in addition to their pictures.

Rebecca Lukens

❧ Old: What's Good About It ❧

Old age isn't for sissies, as Mae West or someone else once said.

Bill Rice and I were busily treading the treadmills in the physical therapy room when we began compiling a list of what's good about it.

- The mortgage is paid off.
- We got the kids through college.
- And they are no longer "the opposition," but our friends.
- They may even be better parents than we were!
- We won't have to admit heating costs are up—not until June 30.
- Gas may be high, but Kroger's is close. And who's going anywhere?
- Some neighbors have higher cholesterol than ours.
- Some neighbors take a bigger handful of morning pills than we do.
- No need for a new wardrobe. Who knows I bought this in the 60s?
- No need to stay home to wait for service men. They always come.
- Cleaning the gutters isn't my worry any more.
- Who misses starting the fire in the fireplace?
- None of our kids are living in the basement. In fact, if they return, they'll first have to dig a basement.

Life is good.

What Wonders!

In the first week of kindergarten, each of my four children gave me a start. A sudden loud outcry: "*Mommy!*" I rush to respond: "*What's the matter, honey?*" The quiet reply: "Just checking!" You'd think I'd learn.

On December 9, 2002, Daniel came home from school with a wad of raffle tickets, a 24-inch string of them, and told Sal that he'd bought them for a good cause—the homeless.

"How much did you spend for that string of tickets?"

"Twelve dollars. They were only 25¢ apiece."

"Twelve dollars!"

"But Mom, it was for a good cause."

"That was your Christmas money!"

On December 13, he told me he hadn't won the big prize for buying the most—some techie thing. But he *had* won two tickets to the Miami women's basketball game. When I said, "They're good. You'll love them," he said, "Well, I gave them to Nick. But if they're good, I'll ask Nick for them back and give them to Dad and Andrea for Christmas."

On December 14, Daniel called to ask if I would take him shopping for a gift for his mom. So I picked him up. As we parked the car, he asked, "Who's paying for this? I lost my wallet. Well, it only had a dollar in it." So we went to the Miami Co-op, where he went right to the dictionary shelves, saying, "We have to be economical about this." Keeping in mind his expenditure for the homeless, I thought this comment was a good sign. We bought a $6 paperback dictionary, went home to my house to wrap it, and he was delighted.

Later in the afternoon, Andrea and her mom came to deliver my huge poinsettia. Andrea saw a sales slip on the table, and, not wanting me to know how much they'd spent on the poinsettia, she picked it up and handed it to her mother—who now knew Daniel had bought a dictionary for her.

On Sunday, December 15, Andrea called to tell me she was ready to take me up on my offer to help her shop for her mother. She wanted a calendar, so we checked it all out at the Co-op, Snyder's, and Walmart. Then, since she was hungry, we stopped at Wendy's for lunch. At my invitation, she used my car phone to call her mom, to tell her we were going to wrap the gift at my house.

"Mommy, we went to Snyder's and their calendars were $20, and to the Co-op, and theirs were $12, and to Walmart where they were $4." Then she gasped. "I just told Mommy about her Christmas gift. And yesterday I told her about Daniel's. I spoiled everything."

"Perhaps she'll forget," I suggested.

Andrea, at about four, was playing with the extra skin on the backs of my hands, and she asked, "Nana, what did you look like when you were new?" I said, "I looked a lot like you." I'm afraid I scared her to death.

On April 10, 2003, Daniel showed me a wonderful stuffed cobra, coiled and ready to strike, a piece of good taxidermy he had bought for $15 at an antique shop. (Mom had loaned him some money.)

I asked him, "Where do you get your money, Daniel?"

"Selling drugs."

The reply is comparable to a reply I got last spring. Daniel didn't want to sign up for the city Rec program at the Tri.

I asked him, "But what will you do all summer, Daniel?"

He replied, "Run the streets."

He can set off the alarms.

Since Andrea's birthday—10—was coming this week, I told her I'd pick her up after school so we could shop for a swimsuit. If I was late, she was to walk to her Mom's office and wait for me there. As I drove down Spring Street, I saw someone taking long strides, dressed in an XXL green t-shirt, wearing a red cap with a peak and a too-big backpack. I drove by and looked back to see if it was Andrea. It was.

In the car she said "No offense, Nana, but I'd really rather go to Mom's office. I haven't been there for a long time. We can get a swimsuit any time." I agreed and our outing never happened.

At Daniel's 12th birthday party, Andrea offered a joke her teacher had told in class.

"This not-very-smart man heard that most traffic accidents happen within ten miles of home. He began to worry. So he moved."

Daniel gave me a high compliment. "I'm glad you're not a boring grandmother."

I took my old answering machine to Sally and told her I had even found the instructions. She said, "Good. I can do it myself. I don't have to wait for Andrea to figure it out for me."

Andrea told me her mom had asked her to wake Daniel. She went to his room, but instead of just calling, "Daniel, wake up!" she touched him on the shoulder. He reached up and hugged her. Then he realized it was his sister, not his mom, and he said, "Aargh!"

She is taking saxophone lessons and played for me: "Aahh (low) Aahh (medium) Aahh (high)." Good start.

She's running for class president. Her ads are computerized— in color.

🔳 Freedom for the Vagabond 🔳

The night Olie pushed out the window screen he discovered Life
in the Big World.

I awoke one morning and couldn't find Olie. I called. I whistled.
I looked. I searched. Not in the utility room where his necessaries
are—food, water, and litter box. Not in the garage—where he'd never
been before so why did I look there? A close examination of the
bedroom, however, showed fresh air at the lower edge of window
screen, allowing room for an agile cat to escape. He was gone.

But one quick whistle at the patio door, and he appeared.

From that moment on, Olie spent hours meowing, crying,
begging, pleading, scratching and pawing at the patio door. "Out!"
he begged. I let him out and in, in and out, time after time, day
after day, each time having to seek my cane, grab the arms of my
recliner, ease to my feet, and hunch to the door. Many times a day.
He verified Garrison Keillor's statement: "A cat is always on the
wrong side of the door."

Neighbor Margaret said she had a cat-door; weary, I checked it
out. Suzanne had a catalog. I ordered a "windoor," one that fits in
the lower half of my bedroom window and when it arrived, showed
Olie how it worked: "Look, you just flip the bottom magnet with
your nose, it opens, and you're out." Olie looked at it suspiciously,

and meowed at the patio door. I repeatedly demonstrated the Cat Exit-Entrance. He looked at it suspiciously, and meowed at the patio door. So I locked his door.

Then the housekeeper came, and with her the vacuum cleaner. Without me to open the patio door, Olie was reduced to trying his Very Own Door. He rubbed it, pawed at it, meowed at it, and pushed it with his nose. It didn't open. He gave up and crawled under the bed.

Finally one day it all worked out. Now Olie leaves promptly after breakfast—before if I open the door—hops out and disappears. Ten minutes later he returns to meow at my knee—just to say he's home—then disappears again. And again. And again. And again. He's never home.

I have to sprinkle catnip on the carpet by my chair to convince him it's worthwhile sticking around, rather than taking off to nap on Margaret's patio table. He's become a vagabond and should never have tasted such freedom.

◙ Being an Escort ◙

When my term on the Planned Parenthood Board ended, I felt a loss of involvement in a cause I regard as vitally significant. When Sue Momeyer, formerly Executive Director of the PP of Butler County and now Director of the larger Tri-State organization centered in Cincinnati, moved to a new home, she invited me to a housewarming party where I was delighted to see old friends, among them Eileen Goldman, director of Oxford PP patient services.

I told Eileen that if there was ever a need for an escort to the Cincinnati clinic where abortion was now available, I'd be glad to drive. That next week the Hamilton clinic called, asking me to meet a young woman at the Hamilton clinic early the next morning. There I saw a young African-American woman, possibly high school age, trying to be inconspicuous as she waited in the shadows. I knew only her first name and I called it out. She quickly slipped into the car, and settled into the passenger seat, her head tucked into her coat collar as we drove out of town. Although she said nothing, from her body language, I sensed total fury.

It seemed strange to have someone sitting so close to me and not be talking with her, so I said quietly, "I'm Becky." No response. To fill the silence, I turned on the car radio and we drove on to the Cincinnati address I'd been given. Unfamiliar with the city, and with the narrow streets at its center, I drove up and down looking for the abortion clinic address. I took several wrong turns, passing the same buildings several times. The silence in the car now became increasingly tense, anger so strong it was oppressive. My passenger was anxious to get this over with—and I could understand that. But here was a "helper" who was totally useless, postponing things, not expediting them. Finally, I found the clinic and was able to park the car. As I recall, the lot was guarded. Inside the small entryway, also guarded, my passenger resentfully told the receptionist her first name and the time of her appointment. Then the outside clinic door was unlocked for us.

State law required that a patient be given the Right-to-Life materials to read before an abortion could be done, and the receptionist gave the required papers to the patient to read during a wait of half an hour or so. Together we waited for her name to be called, and during this silent time, I suddenly realized that she must have had to sneak out of her house early and silently, and perhaps was hungry. She said she was, and I handed her several dollars for the vending machine. She took the money and said "Thank you," her first words to me, then found some packaged food and a Coke and quietly ate a delayed but odd breakfast.

While she was in seeing the counselor or nurse, I read the abhorrently illustrated Right-to-Life materials in the waiting room. Unable to concentrate, I looked around me. An attractive, well-dressed woman in her thirties sat opposite me, and I thought how the need *not* to bear a child has numerous reasons, and although the process was legal, and financially available, privacy might not be. Perhaps, rather than search for a private doctor who would help, she knew Planned Parenthood provided all she needed—legality, expertise and privacy.

My passenger touched me on the shoulder when she finally returned and said nothing but, "I'm ready." As we left the building, we passed the protesters on the sidewalk, trying to shame us with their taunts. She held her head up and we began our quiet trip home to Hamilton. This time I felt a need to talk to her and said, "I understand unwanted pregnancy, and I think you've done the right thing." She snarled an answer: "I couldn't have another one."

As I recall, she said her mother was taking care of the first baby, and that was enough. Her anger was so strong that I imagined my passenger as the victim of a ruthless father or brother whose baby this was. The intensity of her fury at being pregnant seemed to tell me that the sex had been traumatic.

But the event was not over for her; by then-current Ohio law, she was required to read the Right-to-Life materials, reconsider for 24 hours, and if she still wanted to go through with it, return the following day. I was terribly sorry to hear that the whole thing was not yet over. The next day I could not be available. (I wonder now what was so important I couldn't postpone it. Surely I could have.)

Fortunately, the clinic had money for the bus, and she promised to go back. Her anger must have been sufficient to motivate her, but I was sorry.

I never saw her again.

My second experience with being an escort was very different.

The clinic in Hamilton called to ask if I could pick up a woman living at the YWCA on Third Street at an appointed early time. When I arrived, a young woman was waiting on the steps for me; she eagerly hopped into my car.

This patient turned out to be very talkative. She announced immediately that an abortion was "no big deal." She'd had one before and it was "easy." I asked if her boyfriend knew, and she said, "Oh, yes. I talked to him last night." I learned that she saw him regularly, that he'd been responsible for her earlier pregnancy, that he already had a child with someone else and was trying to get custody. Would she see him again? Yes, she said, she'd see him again when he called. He loved her. Being "loved," I realized, was what she craved; so great was her need that she'd permit him to do whatever he wanted with her body. And her future. I encouraged her not to talk with the boyfriend, and to refuse to see him again. No doubt my comments fell on deaf ears.

This story sounded to me like that of a totally irresponsible woman and an exploitive man, and the longer I listened to her, the more certain I was that my passenger probably was of below average mentality, and probably unemployable. She was clean but slovenly. She told me she was happy at the Y where she lived, I surmised either on a meager SSI disability income, or as a ward of the state. Although I spoke briefly to her about the common sense of an abortion, and asked what she would do with a child to support, she apparently had given little thought to the risk of unprotected sex. There seemed to me nothing I could do at this point but listen and take her to the clinic.

This address was also new to me, but in the same general area of Cincinnati. We finally found the small clinic hidden in a congested area near the University. This time we were met at the clinic by several protesters waiting on the public sidewalk, carrying placards and taunting us, trying to shame her for "killing her baby" and me for helping her. We had both been instructed never to respond to a protester, but I had to restrain her from starting an argument there on the street. She talked back to them. "It's legal. I've done it before and I know it's not against the law." I urged her on to the front door where a policeman stood watch. He held the door for us to enter a small, enclosed porch where my patient gave her name and appointment time. The receptionist then unlocked the door and we entered a small waiting room.

Others waited there—a solemn mother with a teenager, for instance. (I thought how lucky the girl was; some parents throw their pregnant daughters out on the street.) My companion then began her tale once again: "Don't worry. It's easy. It won't hurt a bit." Fortunately these sad and embarrassed people did not reply. To them this was nothing to chat about, nor to brag about, but an agonizingly solemn experience after a decision made in anguish.

On the way out, the protesters on the sidewalk reminded us that we had done something terrible, but now my patient was more subdued. In the car, I learned more. "The doctor," she said, "talked to me." He told her she shouldn't use abortion as a method of birth control. He suggested that this man was not treating her fairly. And if she wouldn't insist he wear a condom, she should take care of her own fertility, by using contraception. Then he asked how old she was. "Sixteen," she said. "I'm sorry," he said, "but you're too young to request an implant" "under my skin." But she could ask the doctor "to do it" when she was 18.

What could I say on the way home? I despaired that she would not change in any way. Despaired that perhaps she *could not* change in any way. Would my inadequate counseling do anything to help her? I'd tried, but I'm doubtful. I wondered if there would be more trips to the clinic before that birthday came.

My last experience as an escort was quite different.

I answered a call from the United Campus Ministry program director and went in to see her. There I learned that a young woman had come in to ask for counseling about pregnancy, and had struggled with the idea of an abortion. She was a Catholic, could not speak with her priest, and had come to the UCM, perhaps thinking that this was as close to a religious counselor as she could get. The counselor sensibly suggested to me that perhaps I "should meet her before arranging transportation."

A day later we met at the UCM office. She was a beautiful young woman, a freshman, I believe. We introduced ourselves by first names, and I told her what I believed, that she was making a wise decision, that she had her life before her. She listened quietly and we agreed that we would meet in front of her dormitory on the appointed date.

When I drove up to the dorm at an early hour, there were no students around, but she sat waiting for me with an attractive African-American boy. She got into the car quickly and introduced me to her boyfriend, a soft-spoken student from another university, who had come for the weekend. I immediately thought appreciatively about the young man's sense of responsibility and his important support for the woman who was bearing the burden of their actions. We talked little, and the car radio covered any conversation they might have had.

This clinic was still another for me to find, tucked away between large buildings close to the Cincinnati hospital enclave. Again we met with protesters, but the three of us said nothing. All went as planned, and we started back to Oxford. This time I observed something new. The young man was eager to talk, but she was not.

Perhaps he felt the understandable male reaction: Brush hands together, and think, "Good. That's over." She, however, was silent. Obviously it was not over for her. Perhaps pondering the significance of what she had done, immense to one devout in the Catholic faith. Perhaps thinking ahead to wanting some day to have a child. Or to her liberal conditioning, the kind we had done at my own house. "Look at African-Americans as human beings like yourselves. They're no different from you. Treat them as you do your other friends."

What would happen to this relationship, I wondered. Would it continue?

I said something about having grown children, and that I was grateful for the legal status of abortion now. I even suggested that "Perhaps you can tell your mother someday. You'll be surprised at her compassion and her loving acceptance." Then I praised her for her courage. These words were spoken out of my own experience and I wanted her to know that.

Several days later I found in my mailbox a note dated the day after the event; it had been addressed to "Becky" at the UCM, and forwarded to me. It was written on pretty notepaper and filled with gratitude. When I told my daughter about the event, she said, "She'll never forget you, Mom." If that's the case, I'm glad.

卍 A Year of Living Ecstatically 卍

When graduate classes were over at Syracuse University, my friend Julie, who was learning how to be a dean of women, and I were too close to New York City to go home to Akron and Fargo. We had to check out the Big City. So off we went. I'm not sure how Julie's parents looked at the venture, but I know my own were trying to be non-committal. Only after several months did Mom write to tell me that the ladies at First Lutheran Ladies Aid wondered "just what *is* Becky doing in New York?"

On arrival, we checked in at the YWCA, looking for temporary housing. It was 1945, and neither of us knew about anti-Semitism—if that's what it was—but Julia Swedenburg (a Swede) and Rebecca Johnson (a Norwegian) were sent to the YWHA, a place we knew nothing about, but finally decided was for those of Hebrew extraction. The YWCA, however, did give us the address of a woman who would rent us a room for a few days, just until we found an apartment.

But first, an income was important. Julie found a job as a tour guide at the War Weapons display in the lobby of the Chrysler Building on the corner of Lexington and Forty-second, a few blocks from Times Square. For work, she wore a sexy khaki uniform and told people proudly how much damage each of the weapons on display would do. I found a job as a receptionist/switchboard operator right across the street from Julie, at Container Corporation of

America. When I walked in and got the job on the spot, I told the office manager that I couldn't start that day, because Julie and I planned to go to the Statue of Liberty on Friday, and perhaps the flea circus on Saturday. But I'd be free on Monday, thank you.

Next, the search for an apartment. We were making fabulous money, $65 a week for me, I remember, far more than my graduate stipend had paid. Since we were now employed, Julie and I had to sandwich our apartment search in at lunchtime or after five. On my lunch hour, I found a wonderful apartment immediately: ground level, in the 80s, with a backyard garden of our own. All excited, I told the landlord I'd be back with my roommate at 5, but I had to check it out with her. At 5:10 Julie and I checked back. It had been taken. We should have known. Housing, we'd been told numerous times, was rent-controlled and very tight, different from Akron and Fargo. One apartment we checked out had a bathtub in the kitchen, with a wooden cover to drag over it at mealtimes. Voila! A kitchen table! Nothing like it existed either in Fargo or in Akron. We snorted and rejected it.

We did find a third floor walk-up at 366 East 66th Street, across from what seemed to be the address of several medical students attending classes at some institution that we either imagined or heard was attached to Cornell Medical School. That was not the determinant for signing the lease, of course; we signed because we were tired of looking and wanted a place of our own.

The apartment actually had bells at the front door! Bells that would ring in the individual apartments, to announce a guest who wished to enter. We could buzz them in! Fargo had nothing like this. Nothing. Even walking up to the third floor was something new. A kitchen behind two skinny closet doors! A living room with two windows looking out on East 66th Street. A tiny bathroom with traditional equipment, a bedroom with not only a fridge but a casement window looking right into the airshaft. Who could ask for anything more?

The next project was finding furniture. In my walks to and from the Lexington Avenue bus stop I noted a sign in a window: "Moving. Furniture for sale." A quick check, and I met the woman who was moving back to Iowa. (Imagine it! Leaving New York!) For twenty dollars we bought twin bed frames with mattresses, plus a third narrow bed, a drop leaf "dining" table, a cardboard chest perfect for an end table, and a dresser with three legs. (Not a problem. The right number of books leveled it up for us.) The furniture-seller threw in a couple pans and a small throw rug, then recommended a drayman who lived down the block. With the help of a wheelbarrow and several trips, he delivered our new furniture. Perfect.

The next problem was curtains for the windows on the street. I went off in search of a fabric store and returned to tell Julie of some great gauzy stuff (like curtains) at four yards for a dollar just down Third Avenue from us. We could afford that. Nice color: kind of burgundy. Julie went off to approve or disapprove, and returned with yards and yards and yards, not of burgundy, but of fire engine red. Thumb-tacked to the top and side window frame, they were sensational. In fact, we noted a week later that our unknown neighbors across 66th Street now had fire engine red curtains. Imitation is the highest form of praise.

Home decorating went on sporadically. That fake fireplace needed a picture over the mantel. Fifty-seventh Street with all its galleries was a few steps away from 420 Lexington, an easy walk at lunch time. I took it on myself to buy a print of a section of a Diego Rivera mural, nicely dominated by reds that matched our fiery curtains. A Newberry dime store frame, 10" x 14", finished it off. When I proudly showed it off to the "boys in the office," salesmen and others, I ignored the comment, "Kind of small for over a fireplace, isn't it?" They hadn't seen the fireplace. Or the effect!

We couldn't leave the beds as they were, two of them uncovered and joined to form an L in a corner of the living room. They were too tacky. We'd make matching spreads. On our neighborhood prowls we'd passed a place that rented sewing machines, and we'd already found the fabric store. Blue chambray tops, and plaid skirts with a line of red, of course, gathered into a boxy effect. Although anxious about the weight of the little Singer, we put it on the drop leaf table. It held, and the tiny portable did the trick. We now had a living room with a corner sofa, not a bedroom. A board across the radiator in the corner made a bookshelf. Next, the footlocker covered in leftover blue chambray made a coffee table. We were in business. It was class! Sheer class!

Now we could explore the Big City. Central Park was a few blocks away, a wonderful forest with walkways and benches, and a pond and a little zoo, and a restaurant we might rarely afford. And people. People for people-watching. We could sit on a bench beside the walk, see couples, and mothers and children, and maids and children, and old men slumped over a checkerboard, and office workers eating their wax-papered sandwiches. Sometimes there'd be a PDA to watch—a Public Display of Affection—and we'd wonder what held this couple or that one together. Or even, if watching was eventful, we'd be intrigued by watching a successful pick-up.

Not only was Central Park a prime people-watching space, but 420 Lex was a few short steps from Grand Central Station where people-watching during lunchtime was sensational. Some people spread out for a nap on an empty bench. Or waited anxiously for a train. Or perhaps just for some human connection. Or they were wandering into a small shop for fried oysters. (Oysters, apparently, were edible.) Sometimes there'd be hasty goodbyes to wonder about, or teary hellos to smile over. Once I saw an unappealing young man sketching me, but wasn't tempted to accept his invitation to be his nude model—even if his room was just around the corner. The invitation wasn't shocking, just funny. Something to tell my roommate about, but not to mention in a letter home.

Julie and I soon heard from my friends from college, Gen and Edie. During my time at Syracuse they had been teaching school in Minnesota. Childhood friend Gen, a Music major, was teaching public school music in a small town on the Iron Range, not far from Duluth. Edie, college roommate and Home Ec major, taught high school sewing and cooking in a little town in southern Minnesota. Neither of them wanted to go back, and persuading them to join Julie and me was easy. When Julie left after the summer to go back to Deaning classes, I'd have company in our red-curtained apartment.

But first I had to get lost looking for Penn Station, their arrival point. I found 34th street all right, but East and West apparently confused me, and I wandered around in the almost deserted streets of what appeared to be factories whose workers had left for home. Some kindly soul must have answered my Traveler's Aid kind of questions, and I caught a cross-town bus to the right address. It was wonderful to see them, and suddenly Julie and I were guiding them around.

Housing four people in our space was a cinch. Two single beds in the living room took care of two, and the single bed in the bedroom (across from the fridge and just under the airshaft window) took two, sleeping head to toe. "Just for the summer, till Julie goes back to Syracuse in the fall." It would be no problem. In fact, we took turns doubling up, good practice for when just the three of us were there in the fall. Later on, when one of us was entertaining a date in the living room, the two extras would go back to head-to-toe sleeping.

But we were invaded. North Dakota is not particularly hospitable to cockroaches: too cold and dry. But we found out what they were. Imagine it. Living in a roach-infested place. I called the landlord. Told him we were disgusted. What was he going to do about it? One day we came home from work to find that there were some strange-looking things lined up along the baseboards. Close investigation revealed these dusty items were slices of potato, each one spread with something strange. An empty bottle labeled J.O. Paste, roach poison, had been left in the wastebasket. Our landlord had invaded us to get rid of the invaders. We had to buy more potatoes, but that wasn't all. He knocked on our door next day; all three of us were there, and he was irate that three of us lived there in his double-occupancy rent-controlled apartment. I'm not proud of it, but I think we must have insisted that one of us was visiting. And in a sense, we all felt temporary for that matter.

◈ Amateur Mothering ◈

Reading an interesting book called *Manhood for Amateurs* by Michael Chabon roused in me some thoughts of how often in my mother role, as well as others, I've done an amateur job. Should I write about them? Clearing them out of my memory by writing them might work as an exorcism.

One incident involves my second son Tom, a helpful cheerful boy who always was ready to give or get a hug. We lived in a tri-level house in Chillicothe, OH, which meant that on entering the front door you were met by a slate floor and a half flight of stairs, with risers painted a dark green. Our only problem was the milk-man's leaving our big milk order out on the front porch, forcing me to carry the heavy glass bottles up the steps to the kitchen. It was a big job—a man's job, we might say. On this day, Tom at six was in a helpful mood. He picked up a gallon bottle, and, as he struggled to hold the screen door open, he dropped it. And of course it smashed to bits on the slate floor, and on up the risers of the stairway.

Instead of thanking him for his efforts, or consoling him for the accident he felt so sorry about and hugging him while he cried, I blew my top. I picked up the glass pieces and went off to find the mop and scrub bucket, then sloshed around till the blackness of the slate floor showed once more. Then I tackled the white milk spots on the dark risers, grousing the whole time.

I wish I could recall holding and consoling him. I hope he remembers that I did. I hope I did.

A second memory of amateur mothering involves my son Jim. We lived on a hill above the central city of Chillicothe; each day Jim walked down a long set of steps to school. One morning before he left, he asked if he could stay after school and play with his friend Billy. I consented and suggested Jim walk to City Hall to ride home with his dad at five.

That evening at the dinner table, Jim was very excited. He described his friend's house, exactly where it was, what they did and how much he liked Billy. After his enthusiastic report and all our interested comments, I was now aware of the neighborhood, and I asked a question that to this day I regret. "Is Billy black?" I asked, not really caring whether Jim's good friend was or not.

My Jim was thoughtful. Then he said, "I don't know. I'll have to look." I had made him recognize skin color as a difference, not as an irrelevance.

Jim is now past sixty; perhaps he has forgotten. I will never forget.

Years later when I was a guest lecturer talking about children's literature at Texas A&M, a student asked me a question: "How come when in your textbook you recommend a fine novel about a close friendship, you never say the girls are of different races? Was it because you didn't think race should matter?"

I might have made my point. But too late for little Jim.

⊞ Signing in Blood ⊞

Life for a younger sister could be pretty exciting, given the structure and personalities of a family.

Sally, serene in any environment, walked or toddled with me during our short life in Birmingham, Michigan. We'd sightsee in the neighborhood, checking gardens and houses and pets as we passed them by. "Mistress Mary, quite contrary, how does your garden grow?" often walked with us. Each time we passed a neighbor's flowerbed, Sally pointed out to me "a garden grow."

As she grew up a bit, she was fascinated by the piano and begged to take lessons, even, when she grew to high school age, taking lessons one summer from Miami Professor David Bean. When she auditioned with him that summer, she answered his question, "Why do you want to be my student?" by telling him she was "tired of taking lessons from the lady across the street." He took her on for the summer; that "across-the-street teacher" must have been adequate.

Often Sara-Sally-Ann quietly got away from the Lukens crowd to the comfort of the piano. At other times she picked up her knitting. In the third grade she won the "hobby prize" for knitting her own sweater.

But one day in her early teens, Sally witnessed her sister Jane's slamming the stairway door and roaring up to their room, where she flung open the window and yelled to the neighborhood: *Stop beating me!"* (She was safe, actually. True, she once called me "a witch," but her father was slow to wrath.).

It may have been this time or earlier, but once when I was doing the tucking-in at bedtime, Sally asked me solemnly, "Would you like me to sign my name in blood that I won't act like Janie?"

She paused a minute, and added, "I better sign now. I may not feel like it later."

🔒 Matching Gifts 🔒

At Christmastime in the year 2000 or so, the Lukens family was gathered for festivities. As usual Janie and Sally, not penniless but a bit short of cash, had asked for ideas for my gift, and as usual I tried to come up with something affordable. From a colleague I had received a catalog of jewelry she was selling. Without knowing prices, I chose some classic hoop earrings and circled the picture in the catalog.

Now, on Christmas Day, we were opening gifts—and surprise!– a small box appeared with my name on it. My turn to open my gifts, and there in its snowy cotton cushion was one golden earring! I exclaimed with delight! I loved it.

Two days later, December 27, we gathered at Sally's house for my birthday. I was wearing my one gleaming earring, and it flashed exotically in honor of the day. Accompanying the birthday cake (chocolate, of course) was a small box with my name on it. Having blown out the multitude of candles, I eagerly approached that box.

Behold! A single gold earring! It matched! And I just happened to have an empty ear lobe ready for it!

It came as no surprise. Once upon a time, I had told Janie and Sally about the Christmas my sister Ruthie and I had each knitted a woolen sock for our Dad to wear with his hunting boots. Down

the leg of my Kelly green sock, I had embroidered "From Becky."
Ruthie had of course embroidered hers with a similar inscription:
"From Ruthie."

Dad's gift was celebrated years ago (almost as much as the tie tack
that looked like he'd buttoned his tie to his shirt). We celebrated
those two golden hoops on my birthday.

❧ a. k. a. Nana ❧

Cleaning up the garden with Andrea is a trip. In my warm jacket, she's quick with the long-bladed trimmer, loves snipping the ornamental grass, clipping the butterfly bush and the purple sage right down close to the earth. When we come in after our work in the cold, she removes her shoes at the patio door, puts the garden tools back where they usually hang on the garage wall, and announces she'd like some tomato soup.

I'm surprised; she just came from lunch with Papa at Westover. But she turns the cupboard's lazy-Susan round and round until she finds a can of beef and veggie soup. She finds a pan, opens the can, reads the directions, and pushes the stove On button to Medium, (not like me: I seem to cook everything on high and later scour the pan.)

Meanwhile, I take a paring knife to the soles of her clean white shoes, dig out the mud in their tread, and rinse them in the laundry tub. Andrea, about to hang up the jacket, discovers on the closet shelf a sheepskin hat with ear flaps, puts it on, pulls down all flaps, admires herself, and is delighted to find she can have it. On seeing Daniel, she is unmoved by his comment: "Nana offered it to me first, long time ago."

As she left, she said, "It's fun working in the garden for Grandma— a.k.a. 'Nana.'"

I told her Grandpa Gross about "a.k.a." and he commented, "She's been reading too many crime novels."

◙ No. Not Running ◙

"He should run for Mayor! Dave Hirsch should." The statement echoes through the Miami Recreation Center, Dave's 6 AM location.

Dave has an infinite capacity for friendship. Once he knows your name, he won't forget it. In fact, he'll probably remember the names of your spouse, your children and where they live now that they've left home. He even stores away the name of the puppy you adopted last summer. If by chance he's forgotten, he'll ask again and he'll record the response in his Retrieval System.

An inveterate moviegoer, Dave often goes to the movies in Oxford, Springdale or Cincinnati. One evening his group of four contemporaries strolled back up the aisle to the exit at Cinema Ten, when suddenly two "old ladies" about his age sitting near the back row—obviously awaiting the moment they could call out to him—stopped Dave in his tracks. "Doctor Hirsch!"

He stopped. The women stood, ready for animated conversation, then followed him out to the lobby. Meanwhile his three movie companions waited, admiring Dave's friendliness as he chatted with his two former dental patients. Finally, feeling it was time to move on, Dave mustered up a parting line: "We must have lunch sometime."

To his three waiting friends, he commented, "Why did I say that? Now I have to set up lunch." A poor closing line.

Two weeks later the same four cinema lovers were again at Cinema Ten. This time as Dave and his three friends entered the lobby, two *different* older women were waiting by the door to the parking lot. To the three movie-going friends it was a familiar scene: "Doctor Hirsch!" A repeat performance, including Dave's "closing line."

A month later the four of us tried another trip to the movies. This time Dave refused to get out of his seat till the theatre was empty.

▣ One-Upmanship Among the Aged ▣

—Finally got an appointment with the orthopedist.

—*When do you go?*

—December.

—*That far ahead? What's it for?*

—Trouble with my knee. Arthritis, I suppose.

—*What's he going to do? Arthroscopic surgery?*

—Who knows?

—*I know about that. They open up your knee socket and scrape out the gunk.*

—You had that? When?

—*While back.*

—How long were you in recovery?

—*You don't want to know, but let me tell you it wasn't easy.*

—Did you try physical therapy beforehand?

—*Yeah. Tried everything. Had a knee replacement later.*

—Wow! Where'd you go?

—*Blue Ash.*

—Way down there?

—*Long way.*

—Who did it? Snyder? I hear he's good. Had back problems first. Decided a neurologist was my next move.

—*Try any pain killers?*

—Yeah, lots. Even tried chiropractic. And a posture regimen called Alexander Technique. Had to drive to Montgomery for sessions.

—*Try acupuncture?*

—Finally drove to Kenwood for it. Thought it was helping, but I was too optimistic.

—*Why didn't you go the NSAID way? Those nonsteroidal anti-inflammatory drugs helped me. Have you tried them?*

—Most of them. All gave me stomach problems.

—*With Vioxx, I guess that's common. Ulcer symptoms for some people. How about Celebrex?*

—Ulcer symptoms.

—*That one, too?*

—Yeah, and a third one, I forget the name. Same story.

—*Well, there's still Mobic.*

—Never heard of it.

—*I guess it's common in Canada.*

—Oh, I remember, I did try that one, too. Used it for a month. No help, did things to my stomach.

—*But you took that stomach stuff with them all., didn't you?*

—I did. Tried them with all the meds. Gave my blood pressure a rocket shock.

—*Are you sure? Never heard of that. Friend of mine tried it, and it helped a lot.*

—Wonder if she had stomach problems, blood pressure problems.

—*I'll ask.*

—Well, I've pretty much given up on NSAIDs. Maybe just rely on Tylenol.

—*Yeah, but only eight a day. That probably won't do it.. How about those glucosamine chondroitin pills? Size of horse pills.*

—Have they ever been evaluated by the F.D.A?

—*Not that I know of, but a lot of people take them.*

—Yeah, ask them if they help and they say they don't know. Say they stay on them. Afraid to stop.

—*How's your cholesterol?*

—Not so good.

—*Statins help with high cholesterol, I hear. But mine's O.K.*

—Lucky you.

—*How high is yours?*

—Low.

—*You're lucky. You should see my records.*

—I hear you can't have cheese.

—*Couldn't live without cheese!*

—*You know, I love Skyline, but I heard that's terrible. . . .*

—Who says? How do you know?

—*Friend of mine went there regularly. One day he asked the waitress about nutritional content. She spoke to the manager; he opened the safe, found the record, and brought it over to his table. Friend's never been back. And he'd eaten "five-ways" all his life! Real sacrifice.*

—Wow! Hope he's O.K.

—*I hate to hear that about Skyline.*

—Did you hear about Marcia's TIA? Yeah, went in last Tuesday. But came home same day.

—*Scared her, I bet.*

—You bet it scared her. Hasn't eaten anything that tastes good since.

—*What's diet got to do with it?*

—Who knows? You just have to do *something*, so you try changing almost everything.

—*Someone told me broccoli and eight ounces of red wine every day helps.*

—Wine's a good idea, but I'd rather drink white.

—*Ever tried the See Food diet? "See food? Eat it!" That's the way I've operated for years. I'm on a new diet—"Tastes good: Spit it out." Gotta go. Check my blood pressure. Doctor says to check it every two days.*

—A real nuisance. Who checks it?

—*Bought myself a blood pressure machine. I try to take it myself.*

—Does that work?

—*Well, it was pretty frustrating. It kept reading EE for Error. So I checked it out with Mike, the pharmacist at Krogers. He tried it on himself. Got a reading. I tried it while he watched. EE showed up again.*

—Strange. I wonder what's wrong with you if you can't take your own blood pressure. You must have something serious.

—*Krogers carries another one with an automatic inflator, sixty bucks. But I already spent forty on this one.*
—Whatcha going to do now?
—*I check it at the store's machine sometimes. Sometimes I get up my courage and ask the nurse over at the health center.*
—They do that, even if you're not a patient?
—*Yeah, they're very obliging, kind. I try not to bother them often.*
—Maybe sixty bucks is a good investment. How high is it now?
—*Way up. Went to 203 over 89 once and I had to tear off to the emergency room. Ended up spending the night at McCullough-Hyde. But that's a long story. I'll tell you about it someday. Now, I gotta go.*
—Okay. See you later at the exercise class. Vicky's good....Say, before you go, did you hear about Sue's cataracts?
—*Cataracts? Really? No! First one or second one? I want to hear, but I'm running late. Just enough time before I see good old Doctor Hunt at 3.*
—I'll hold the story. I know you'll want to hear about Daniel's portfolio.

◙ Daniel's Portfolio ◙

October 21, 2008

Dear Daniel,

I am so pleased that you're going to put together a portfolio to submit to the Miami Art Department. That sounds just great.

You probably think that a lot of what you've done is good, but a lot of it isn't good enough. I just want to add my twenty-cents to your choices.

I have several things here, gifts that you have generously given me over the years since Grandpa Gross and I were so excited about what you were doing. All by yourself. A "little boy" at some point.

I have the two portraits you did of the black artist, and I think they are very good, and if you knew what age you were when you did them, it would show a Portfolio Judge how long you've been drawing. At that point you were copying, and perhaps you know that that's how the Great Artists began. They used to be apprenticed to a known artist and work with him (usually a him). Sometimes, after they showed some talent, the Great Artist would even let his apprentices finish a work he had started. That was part of learning. Then, as they improved, they began to do things themselves. (I took art lessons when I was in middle school; I think Andrea has a picture of some tulips I copied in class.)

Another gift I have from you is a Conversation Piece: The wire "Nana" which you did when you were just in grade school shows imagination and skill, too. Anyone who asks about it is surprised that *you* did it, not your mom. Another piece of evidence that you began early to show ability. I wish I knew how old you were when you did that.

The shoe you did in class and that so pleased your art teacher immediately pointed out to her your ability. Another piece of evidence that you have been growing and improving all the time.

And that ceramic piece, the black and white bowl you made by the coil method, is stunning. The choice of shape (not the usual cup-like bowl) calls attention to itself as something unusual, and the use of black and white in such large shapes adds to its beauty. The simplicity of both shape and design is what makes it a handsome piece.

And the next thing I have—and love—is the small pot/vase you threw on the wheel. As you know, I showed it to the retired ceramics professor who lives here at the Knolls, and he immediately commented not only on its perfect shape and its thinness, but on your use of glaze. He kept it for a while and then told me, "Encourage him."

Daniel honey, you've been doing unusual work for several years, some of it from models, but much of it from Daniel Randolph

Christman's imagination. I hope you'll include much of it in your portfolio. I'd be proud if these things were shown to the Art Department at Miami who are judges.

Besides that, honey, I love you.

~Nana

❧ "Vic and Sade" and Us ❧

Gen and I always listened to "Vic and Sade" on the radio. After a program, we'd roar with laughter on the phone about the couple's inanities. They'd tell a long and uneventful story about Uncle Edgar, pause, and conclude, "He did that.... Later died."

When Vic asked son Rush where he'd been, Rush said, "Down at the Y, watching the fat man play handball."

When they sat on the porch and heard the phone ring, one of the three would say, "Tel'phone's ringing.... Tel'phone's ringing." Sounds of some foot-shuffling. Then again, "Tel'phone's ringing." Finally one of the three—Vic, Sade, or Rush—would get up to answer.

My children sadly had no access to "Vic and Sade," but they adopted the same policy: "Tel'phone's ringing. Tel'phone's ringing." A long wait for foot-shuffling to start before I got up to answer it.

It was always for one of them.

Rebecca Lukens

🔳 Some Day They'll Wonder... 🔳

It's early to think about this, but I do, every time I clip a recipe, and tuck it into my recipe box, either the yellow one or the tan one. Some day my daughters will be checking through them, knowing there'll be nothing there they want, but wondering why in the world I had all these recipes. They won't be scrapping over "Mom's Old Favorites," because they have their own recipes for spaghetti and meatballs and Sunday's baked chicken. They'll just be curious. "Why didn't Mom make all these good ones. We could have used some variety." I can hear them now:

"Listen to this. Anise Toast. Toast that takes some 'making' and doesn't just pop out. Imagine beating eggs and sugar and anise and flour and baking it all, cutting it up, baking it again! For toast?"

"Get this: Oatmeal Cake. With a topping that 'just runs off but is good anyway.' Funny. Why bother?"

"Pumpkin Bread with 11—no, 12—ingredients. For bread? You pour the batter into *four* empty soup cans and bake *four* little breads. Why'd Mom never do this? We could each have had a little loaf of our own. Fun."

"Scones for an English Tea. Never *heard* of an English Tea at our house. She always had her Norwegian coffee at the kitchen table. A tea party? Scones? She knew how to *make* scones? And she didn't!"

"Banana bread! Banana bread comes in a mix box. But apparently it's possible to make it from scratch! Two kinds of flour, two kinds of leavening agents. And lots of work: *Mashed* bananas and *grated* lemon rind and *chopped* nuts, *squeezed* lemon juice? No wonder she never made this. I don't remember it anyway. Maybe she did it for company. I can do it, too. Just give me the box."

"Best Bran Muffins. She cut this one off the Bran Flakes box. No need to stow it away in her private recipe box. It's always there on the box. She must not have noticed."

"Boy, she must have valued this one. She copied Monkey Bread out in ink. Actually, it begins with easy stuff, a tube of butter-milk biscuits cut into 160 pieces *(160!)* Dumped (now there's a real word) into a Bundt pan. Did Mom have a Bundt pan? Don't remember it. You remember any Bundt cakes?"

"More Monkey Bread. And another copy, from the newspaper. Nancy Reagan's Monkey Bread. She didn't even *like* Nancy Reagan and her simplistic "Just Say No" campaign. This sounds compli-cated. Listen: 'Whisk, stir, knead, turn out, knead again, sprinkle, work in.' You want this one, Janie? Too much work for me. I bet Nancy never made it herself."

"Did Mom ever marinate mushrooms? Not that I recall. Listen to this: oil, vinegar, chives, green onions, lemon juice, Worcestershire, browning sauce, prepared mustard, and a pound of washed and dried mushrooms. Too complicated. Toss it."

"No, it might be kind of different." [Sara tosses. Janie experiments.]

"This one takes the cake. What is it? Scrap of paper, torn corner at the top, no title. Just a list.

'(Torn corner) ketchup

1 cup brown sugar

1 teaspoon Worcestershire

1 lb bacon cut in bits

2 8-oz cans water chestnuts

Toothpicks.'

"I can guess what it is. But how *much* ketchup?"

"You know? Mom could have been a good cook. She had a lot of recipes."

⚜ Changing the Parking on Chestnut ⚜

I moved into 611 East Chestnut Street during the summer, delighted that I could walk to my Miami office, although I knew it would be a while before my house was habitable. Chestnut Street was moderately busy at about 8 a.m. and again at 5 p.m. But during the day, I could see the Rinehart's neatly kept house across the street. And down the block a little way Lloyd and Alberta Ittel kept another tidy place. On the south, my lot ended at Chestnut Lane, and a bit farther on lived an old friend and colleague, Frank Jordan.

The remodeling of 611 was a long and complicated process, and intriguing, but as August moved into mid-month, many cars were parking in front of my house. Not bumper to bumper, but a dense row from my driveway to Chestnut Lane.

"Why all the cars, suddenly?" I asked Frank. "Oh, it's the students coming back to town. It'll be that way all year." All year? Excited about the happenings at 611, I wasn't troubled. My hedge would shut them out.

But when classes began, cars parked closer and closer together. Then bumper-to-bumper. Car stereos blared and wheels screamed as student drivers came around the corner from Maple Street. Occasionally metal met metal, and a shower of glass hit the street, as well as on the sidewalk below my hedge. But the house, oriented toward the back deck built around a huge maple tree, was great.

Thanks to neighbors' calls, police marked tires and checked again during the day. They issued parking tickets, some abandoned on my lawn or in the gutter, but a car left there during winter break accumulated tickets. I suggested to neighbors that perhaps the Admissions Office had new rules: "Two cars per student, or no admission to our hallowed halls."

Getting onto Chestnut became difficult as sight lines made edging out impossible. An activist citizen brought a petition around: "Restrict parking on Chestnut Street." No action. Neighbors gathered for Oxford Council meetings, some highly vocal in their protests. "It can't be that bad," was council consensus. Finally, the mayor suggested that council members visit our block next Tuesday to see for themselves.

Neighbors gathered. A suggestion: "Park your cars on the street, bumper-to-bumper. If your car is big, a station wagon or pickup truck, be sure it's at the very edge of a driveway. Leave no spaces."

When council members came, the street was walled in with cars. Students streamed down Chestnut. The mayor seemed surprised. He pulled into a driveway, got out to look, then tried to back out onto Chestnut. Visibility being what it was, he was lucky he wasn't hit. He got out again, wiped his brow, and was convinced.

Council passed a new ordinance: Parking on Chestnut Street became restricted.

◙ Money and Guilt ◙

As I've mentioned, it wasn't easy starting a law practice during the Depression. We lived in three different houses that first year or two, perhaps because of too high rent, I'm not sure. Dad faithfully went to the office each morning, but I had the impression, gathered from somewhere, that there was little happening. When he came home for dinner, we learned that he had had a bowl of soup or a piece of pie and a cup of coffee at the Herbst Department Store cafeteria next door. He might mention having had lunch with Pete Garborg, or meeting someone new, but things were very quiet.

When we had come to Fargo in 1930, I gather he had looked for office space and found a walk-up office at 10 ½ Broadway, over a store downtown, near the Northern Pacific railroad station. (An office at a number with a half sounded far more grand than our mere 1033 Fourth Street North.) As I later understood, the office was rented to him by Pete Garborg, an attorney who was elected to the North Dakota state legislature and therefore gone a good bit of the time. Pete asked him to "take care of things" while he was in Bismarck for the sessions; Dad could also use his law library. During those months Dad had legal work to do.

One of Pete's clients was Lars Christianson, a wealthy Norwegian immigrant who owned the building and some farms, and whose son managed a liquor store for Lars. Because Dad got things done promptly, something I gather that Pete had not been doing, Lars told Dad that he'd like to turn all of his legal work over to him. I remember overhearing a long and earnest discussion with Mom over the issue: Should he do this? Take Pete's client? A second part of the earnest talk concerned the fact that some of Lars's wealth came from a shameful source: a liquor store frequented by drunks and Mexican migrants down in the tacky part of town where we were forbidden to go, the neighborhood close to the Front Street bridge across the Red River to Moorhead, Minnesota.

To Dad and Mom, probably more to Mom since her mother was a WCTU member and a crusader, liquor store profits were not nice. In fact, Mom had told me how Grandma Peterson with other crusaders had gone into a "blind pig," a back room behind a store in Pelican Rapids where alcohol was available. So earnest was she with her kerosene can and her threats to drop it on the pot-bellied stove unless they shut down—killing herself and other crusaders no doubt—that she and her fellow crusaders were success-ful. (Perhaps that meant that Grandpa Peterson was susceptible to such temptation.)

But Lars Christianson seemed to be a member in good stand-ing at First Lutheran Church, and that may have made the differ-ence. Apparently Pete agreed to it because politics interested him far more than his law practice. So Lars, who put Dad on a retainer, became Dad's first real client. That must have meant a great deal to a man with four dependents and small income. (Lars was the first one I had ever heard of who bought his reading glasses at the "five and dime," although later, at the suggestion of my ophthalmologist, I bought them there myself.) Throughout Lars's long life, mutual respect characterized the relationship, and I often heard Dad express his gratitude aloud to Mother or to Lars himself for such substantial help.

Lars's trust in Dad brought in other clients, some on retainers. One family in particular I remember. Two sisters had inherited a lot of land in the state. One sister was single and I gather not quite right in the head; the other was married to a huge lazy man who pretty much turned over management of the farms to Dad. They took long car trips to see the West, and on their return all they talked about was miles-to-the-gallon and miles-per-day, matters far more interesting and impressive than the Grand Canyon apparently. Mom and Dad remembered them at Christmas each year with a big box of many kinds of Norwegian cookies, all of them butter-rich and labor-intensive. One afternoon when they dropped off the Christmas box, the husband ate the whole boxful before the women got home. In a rare burst of disgust, Mom was vocal on the subject.

Membership at the biggest Lutheran church in town—one of several, of course—may also have added to the client list. But to be honest, this was the *Norwegian* Lutheran church where we of course belonged—rather than the Danish, Swedish or English congregations. The Garborgs were also members and I recall no resentment. (Pete's hospitable wife Sophie was a redhead with a henna rinse who "bobbed" her hair when it became fashionable. To Mom, Dad recounted with glee that Pete, as he woke up beside her that first morning of short hair, had said to her, "You better get out of here before my wife gets home." In all innocence I thought that was hilarious, not to know your own wife.)

The law practice must have grown slowly, however, even with help from Lars. On North Fourth Street, we lived across the street from Art Steen and his wife Alice. Art, Dad's St. Olaf roommate, worked for the Chevrolet dealer in Fargo and was on salary while Dad struggled with a small and irregular income. One evening I heard Mom in tears. She was telling Dad that Alice had told her, "If I hear from you one more time that you 'can't afford it' ——" That overheard conversation made a deep impression on me. But at the same time, Dad seemed to me to be very generous, quietly putting a whole dollar bill in the church offering as the plate went by. "Bread upon the waters returns manyfold," I'd been told.

Money was tight. We were given a weekly allowance, a nickel that moved up to a dime when we got wealthier. Of the few pennies, I was to give two or three cents to Sunday School, spend one or two, but save the rest for college—something unknowable lying dimly ahead in the even dimmer future.

Later, when in junior high school, I took the bus from Fargo to St. Paul to visit Aunt Inga, Uncle Albert, and cousin Don who was ten or more years older than I. Don had a paper route and was rolling in wealth. We went to the neighborhood movie one night, he and I, and he was surprised that I had no spending money with me. (The movie was "It Happened One Night" with Clark Gable and Claudette Colbert, squeaky clean as far as I could tell, but Don told Aunt Inga he was afraid I was too young for it.) Because I was embarrassed at having no spending money, I wrote Dad asking if he could send me some. A letter came back. Opening it, I expected to find a quarter, but there was a whole dollar, and enclosed with it a note from Dad warning me about spending it carefully. So, fraught with guilt about my greed, I returned to Fargo a week later and handed him the dollar, intact. I think Dad felt bad.

Even back in North St. Paul, I had known about how tight money was. When I was six or so, Mom once sent me to the store in the next block for some small purchase, telling me that no, I couldn't spend a penny on myself, but must bring home all the change. I knew it was stealing, but on the way home I spent a penny for a gumball in the machine at the gas station. Mom scolded me, and when Dad came home he made me sit for an eternity on the upholstered toy box under the kitchen window while I watched the kids outside playing.

That training in frugality has stood me in good stead all my adult life. When Dad died at 83, he left two-thirds of his estate to charity, and the remaining third in trust for the three of us. As Bob and I sat in the attorney's office and heard the terms of Dad's will, and that the bank would mail each of us a check for $450 each month, Bob was angry: "He died still not trusting his grown children with money."

I was grateful for the money, particularly when I returned from the Fargo funeral to Hamilton a few days before Christmas, and on New Year's Eve learned that Randy had lost another job. My meager "woman's salary" at Miami would have to keep the two of us, mortgage and all, as well as keep Sally in college. After long thought, I wrote the lawyer handling Dad's estate, told him that once again my family and I were going to have to struggle, and asked if that $450 could be increased? In my letter I apologized for appearing greedy, and told him the above story about returning the dollar bill, some sort of apology for my greed perhaps.

Bob was curious as to why Dad had settled in the will on $450 as the monthly payout. I wondered if it had anything to do with a phone call months earlier in which Dad had asked me about the dollar amount of our Hamilton mortgage. Knowing Randy's job history, he may have settled on "an allowance" that would keep a roof over our heads. It did help. A lot.

Church was very important to new immigrant communities, and that was where both Mom and Dad had grown up. As Dad and Mother had, we went regularly to Sunday School, and I even had a time of teaching a class, perhaps when I was in high school. (I give credit to SS for my knowing Biblical allusions.) Each Sunday we got a Sunday School paper with moralistic stories and the Bible story of the day, something to read during the eternal sermon in the long 11 o'clock service we all attended. One story I recall was about a little girl who felt sorry for another child who needed clothes; she decided to give one of her own outgrown dresses, but first she selfishly cut off all the pretty buttons. That seems to have been a powerful story; my classmate Gen recalled it when we met for a reunion in our 50s.

Dad had trouble staying awake during church services, perhaps because he didn't think much of his St. Olaf classmate Reverend Berge who was our minister—whose wife, incidentally, called him "Reverend Berge" too, except when she relaxed and called him just "Berge." When we got home, Dad might comment over the dinner table on some word mispronounced in the sermon—"dezision" being one of them.

When I was small, I went to Junior Missionary Society on Saturday afternoons. I remember nothing about those meetings except that I had to yield up a few pennies for the offering—for support of the missionaries overseas, no doubt. And the fact that Gen was the treasurer one year, and one day she lost all 17 cents on the way home. Disaster!

Far more significant for me, and perhaps for others, was catechism class. When we were in about the sixth grade, we began a two-year-long Saturday morning instruction conducted by Rev. Berge. Our text was *Luther's Small Catechism* as condensed by Pontoppidan. After our confirmation, we signed a little card on the first Sunday of the month, and took it to the sacristy, the office of Rev. Berge, who solemnly asked if we were truly sorry for our sins, placed his benevolent hand on each head, and said a little blessing or something, then let us go back to the front pews. We then could take communion.

After two years of classes, we were confirmed; we could be forgiven, only to sin again immediately in some unknown weakness. Like perhaps having written in the hymnal "go to page 67," then "to page 123," and "to page 451" for a little game for someone else to play during next Sunday's boring times. All very solemn and a bit scary.

My memory of the catechism was that no matter how you looked at it, the whole matter of faith was that of guilt and blame, and forgiveness was essential even if you didn't know what you'd done wrong. Just for example, I remember asking in class—though I wonder how I dared—what the word "adultery" meant; the answer was so veiled that I concluded that any sexual thought was sinful, although I didn't know what sex was at this point.

Speaking of guilt, Grandma Peterson visited us periodically. When Grandpa died, I believe she went around visiting her children. I have a hunch that each visit was not very long, but each one *felt* eternal. Her severity was apparent in her appearance as well as in her sour face and her failure to laugh. (I marvel now at how wonderful Mom's laugh was, so hearty and spontaneous. It must have been in spite of her childhood and thanks to Dad.)

Grandma visited in summer some years, in winter others. In the summer, a revival tent was set up in a vacant lot on Broadway, not too far from the church and the hospital. Revival meetings were perhaps sponsored by several Protestant churches, but I do know that Grandma wanted to go, and I had to go with her. The bouncy gospel hymns were fun to sing, but it was hot inside the big tent, and up front was a sweaty minister waving his shirt-sleeved arms and being vigorous with his call to the penitents to come down front and be saved.

The effect was overpowering. Many went down to the front, and it took a mighty force of will to stay in my chair, guilty as I was of all kinds of anger and resentment at even having to be there, of hating my brother or sister, and being therefore a murderer, for example.

Those were powerful meetings. Perhaps Grandma knitted all through them; she never went down to the front. Perhaps she was there as my chaperone; she was already saved and I was the one who was supposed to hear and respond to the message. My impression, however, was that although my tent-meeting salvation might have been Grandma's agenda, it was not that of either of my parents. They just knew she wanted to go and didn't want to go themselves.

Across the street lived Betty Parries, who went to a Catholic school, to Friday night confession and to a mystery called "Mass." From her I learned that "it counts" even if you were late to Mass as long as you were present "before the gospel." I envied her: She could cancel all guilt for bad things she'd done during the week by merely confessing to a priest in the dark.

To a guilt-ridden, Grandma-Peterson-and-Grandpa-Johnson influenced child, omissions were as bad as commissions. A once-a-week confession to clean the slate for an unseen authority sounded heavenly. I later learned from friends, my students and my reading, that a Catholic child might have to invent sins just to cover all bases—in case she'd forgotten anything. But I also decided that I could never trust what Betty told me, because if she lied, her sin could be canceled so easily.

Her brother Bud was Bob's age; I thought he was a real Clark Gable without the mustache. Once Bud dropped a quarter on the ground, paperboy earnings, and I wrestled him for it; I knew I couldn't keep it, but the wrestling was exhilarating. Besides, there was something forbidden about "liking" a Catholic. Betty and her sister Lynette had movie magazines around the house—something I hadn't known existed—and told me I looked like Joan Crawford. As I look back on my pudgy childhood pictures, that was stretching it a bit, but what it did for my mirrored grimaces was interesting.

⚘ Teaching on the Branch Campus ⚘

When Miami opened its branch campuses, I thought about my commute to Oxford, summer and winter, traffic or none, ice, snow, or sunshine. Should I take the suggestion of our English Department chair, and teach where I lived—in Hamilton? I thought about it, but decided against it. My reason seemed sensible at the time. As it was, wherever I went, I was told about a hole in the street in front of a citizen's house. Or a fire hydrant that shouldn't be there. Or trash that had been missed by the pickup men. Or street lights that shone in a bedroom window.

Apparently I was to relay this information to my husband, Hamilton's city manager. But I had other things to tell him: "The dryer needs repair." "I think the Maytag is on its last legs." "Second son is up for detention at junior high." " Elder daughter is concerned about making sponsor at Taft." If I taught at Miami/Hamilton, these housewifely complaints would be nothing compared to those from parents dissatisfied with their Miami/Hamilton teacher of freshman composition.

But one day I relented and took on an "overload" class in Freshman Comp on the Hamilton campus. It was a delight. At this time, most Hamilton students were grown-ups, some holding down forty hour jobs and taking night classes, some housewives wanting something other than chores, some eager to finish bachelor's degrees interrupted by marriage, and some thinking beyond the years of stay-at-home child care to the possibility of added family income. Others were Vietnam veterans returning to civilian life.

There were ups and downs. Some needed corrections in basic rules of grammar or punctuation. The semicolon was a mystery. Some, to my dismay, hadn't kept abreast of national news and weren't sure who Martin Luther King was. (We read "A Letter from Birmingham Jail" and some had no memory of King's arrest.) Some had never read a whole book. (For one vet I brought a copy of *The Catcher in the Rye* and the next week, he asked, "Are there more books like this one?") One whose writing was poor reported me to the campus director as prejudiced against epileptics. One threatened to report me to a popular radio disc jockey who would broadcast my unfair grading to the world. But I still loved it.

◙ Astonishing Behavior ◙

I had the most unusual experience last week.

In the laundry room I discovered three pairs of slacks, all my size, hanging neatly on hangers, apparently newly washed, and perhaps waiting to be ironed. Or pressed. I wasn't quite sure.

On the back of the utility room door I found hanging something I recognized as an ironing board. By lifting it a bit, I could remove it from the door, and, pushing the door open with my knee, I managed to move the awkward thing through the doorway into the dining area. There I tugged down one end of a metal structure so that the board might open enough to stand steady on the floor. Unfortunately, the other end of the infrastructure was the active end, but once I realized that, I was able to set it upright.

But where did I use to keep the iron that accompanied the board? A quick look around the utility room revealed an iron standing on end atop the fuse box, high on the wall. A long black wire led from the iron once around the box and adjacent to the wall. The cord had a familiar looking thing on the end, and once I'd lifted it all down, I recognized a rectangular plate on the dining room wall not far from the ironing board. They looked similar.

I plugged the cord end to the little plate and waited. Several minutes. I did recall a red light that used to appear on the iron when it was hot. I checked the dial on the handle and found it was properly pointed toward "steam." A few additional minutes made no difference to the red light, however. I checked once again. This time I noticed a dial on the top of the iron with words on it: "silk, wool, cotton, linen, synthetic." Aha! The dial could be moved. I set it on "synthetic." That did it. The light came on.

Once, a long time ago, I had bought a pressing cloth from the Fuller Brush man. Wonder of wonders. There it was. All neatly folded under the box of cat-flea medicine. It was ripped here and there, permanently creased elsewhere, but I spread it out over my polyester slacks. But which side up? There must be a right and wrong. Stains? Top side, of course. With the iron steaming by now, I started off. It felt familiar, like I'd done it once before.

Three pairs of slacks. And now to put it all away. I think there used to be a Magic Button somewhere that would collapse the ironing board. I ran a hand along the underside of the understructure, and as my fingers hit a lever-thing, it collapsed nicely.

Big Day. I can still iron. I may try it again.

◉ Try a Cane! ◉

And finally ...

If you're losing faith in human nature, there's an easy solution: Carry a cane. People come out of the woodwork to assist you. They open doors, offer an arm, ask if they can help, inquire, "Are you all right?"

One January day, I ventured out to the Miami Co-op on the High Street corner, and parked my car on the side street. I soon left the bookstore for my car, but as I crossed the intersection, I felt my cane slip on the icy cobblestones. I didn't fall, but apparently a truck-driver thought I might. Immediately he stopped his huge semi-truck, and leaving the engine running and his driver-side door open, he got out. Without a word, he came over and offered his arm, then walked me back to my parked car. I smiled at him and gave him my earnest thanks: "If ever you lose faith in humanity, just carry a cane. You'll discover how eager people are to help."

One six-footer who opened a door for me said, "It's not the cane. It's my Boy Scout training." But not everyone is/was a Boy Scout.

The other day I needed gas, so I drove up to the Kroger pumps. Ahead of me in line was a young man whose car was attached to the pump by means of the gas hose. Meanwhile, he was busily wiping his car windows clean. He waved apologetically. Through my open window, I called to him: "For a nickel tip, would you do that for me, too?"

"Sure," he said and drove off–to park his car in the lot. A minute later he reappeared, saying, "You thought I wouldn't do it, didn't you?" I replied, "Not really. I've discovered something: If ever you lose faith in human nature, just carry a cane. You'll find how wonderfully helpful people are."

He smiled. "I didn't see your cane. I saw your white hair."

PS: I haven't mentioned marching in Columbus for the ERA! (*My mother, a high school principal, couldn't vote, but never marched.*)

PPS: I'll add stuff in the margins of my published copy. If Henry James could, why can't I? I'll never quit!

❧ MARGINALIA ❧

Rebecca Lukens

◙ Table of Contents ◙

🔹 Louisa May and Me 🔹

Ever since the day I found *Little Women* in the Fargo Public Library, I've dreamed of being a writer, not just "writing," but "being a writer." I dreamed of having my own writing-place (perhaps even in an attic like Jo March's) so I'd be uninterrupted in my creativity. Everything Louisa wrote, including *Jo's Boys, Eight Cousins, Little Men* and anything else with the Alcott name, was for me essential reading.

In college, I wrote papers. In fact, I was so eager to start writing my thoughts down that my assignments were turned in early. The next day, I'd think of something else to add—but too late. The paper was already in the professor's hands. Next, my applications for graduate school were accompanied by some of my early literary efforts, often a bit of "poetry." When at Syracuse University I searched for a thesis topic, my final choice concerned the changes necessary to turn a novel into a play for theatrical performance.

Next, degree in hand, I was close to New York City, "hub of the universe." I left Syracuse for NYC to try several "nothing jobs," clerk in a bookstore, switchboard operator. When things were quiet in the office, I silenced the buzzer so I could write in my journal, "Living in New York." (Slight interruption in my efficiency, of course, when I ignored the switchboard light that took the place of the now-silent buzzer. Once I connected the boss to himself on his own extension.)

At last I found a position on the editorial staff of Funk and Wagnalls *Encyclopedia for Children*. There I not only checked the factual accuracy of entries, but wrote some pieces of my own. But by now it was time for some kind of Real Life (or so my parents seemed to think), life beyond the excitement of the Big City. As an instructor of public speaking at St. Olaf College (I'd been a debater and orator in college,) my yearning to write took a break while I had great fun in the classroom.

Next, marriage took most of my time. In Fairborn, there were soon four kids to read to. I read and read, sometimes just to the four, but occasionally on our front steps to my four plus their poor, deprived neighborhood friends who sprawled on the grass. As I read book after book, I occasionally thought, "This is poorly written," or "This is terrific," or "I ought to try this." Later, in Chillicothe, Ohio, a group of AAUW women organized a writing group. Our monthly meeting required that I produce something to read aloud, and I became a bit more earnest. An obscure journal of Appalachian tales accepted two mediocre tall tales for children. I was hooked!

Our move to Hamilton took me close to Miami University. And of course I exploited my vast teaching experience: My year of teaching public speaking at St. Olaf, plus one semester teaching composition at N.Y. State College in Albany. (I had been fired when I got pregnant. Not good for students to see a pregnant woman in the classroom.) Plus my vast experience at the children's encyclopedia, and two questionable children's stories. Miami "needed" me to teach teachers about children's literature as they entered careers of teaching the "baby boomers." (I had thoughtfully contributed four boomers to that demand.) There were no graduate degrees in Literature for Children at the time, so I was thought to be qualified. My writing had finally paid off, not in royalties but a job.

Without training in the field, I searched for a textbook, but found only disappointment. The most popular textbook was merely plot summaries; the second choice was an anthology of selected chapters from children's books—chapters that might be the best ones from mediocre books. One anthologized chapter, thought I, was inadequate for judging a whole book. I wanted to exercise my own judgments about books.

Then one day in Upham Hall, the Promotion and Tenure Committee of the English department met to consider such frightening possibilities as tenure or firing. A senior professor walked out of the committee room and encountered me, a lowly untenured Instructor. He said, "Your teaching evaluations are good, but—you have to publish."

Academic publishing! Where? No academic journals were interested in what I might write. But maybe *Parents'* Magazine would accept an article about the delights of Mother Goose? And another about reading aloud to children? What else? Write a column? For the Hamilton *Journal*? Maybe. So I offered the editor a weekly column about the only thing I knew. My title, "Children's Books Reviewed," was drab and unimaginative, but the paper got it free, and it forced me to write. Gathering together a few of these columns, I submitted them to *The National Observer*, a weekly newspaper published in New York. They published the column for a short time—until the editor I worked for took sick leave.

I'd have to write the perfect textbook for my class. Such a task seemed overwhelming. Maybe I could just try a sample chapter. Science fiction did not interest me, but good fantasy did. So I began by writing an article contrasting science fiction with fantasy. Because in those days science fiction for children was just getting started, finding poorly written examples was an easy task. Fantasy, however—long the bailiwick of British writers steeped in folk tales of ethnic groups—was a well-established genre. It was easier therefore to find acceptable fantasy. North America was catching up, and high fantasy would soon find an eager readership.

Sampling the publishing market—how to do that? I'd send out a sample of my writing, and ask if the idea interested a publisher. Because Scott Foresman was publishing college textbooks for elementary education students, I mistakenly thought, "No point in querying them. They already do that." I soon found that Houghton

Mifflin and other houses had no interest. One of them, however, suggested that I send my proposal and my sample chapter to Scott Foresman. I did.

This was their field; they found my chapter interesting, and wanted to see a prospectus. What did I anticipate my textbook would include? What did my book do that other texts did not do? Why did anyone need this book more than others already available? In other words, who and what would the competitors be? I knew my competition, and put together my proposal. Eagerly I sent it off.

At this point we were living in an apartment in Columbus, Ohio; our four children had left home for college and adult life, and I lived in a rented a room in Oxford during the work week. Thanksgiving vacation began on Wednesday evening, and as I parked my car in the apartment parking lot, I was eager to see my returning children. Janie came running out. "Mom! Scott Foresman just called! They're going to publish your book!"

Miracle! The weekend was total euphoria.

When Janie and I went to Krogers to do our Thanksgiving dinner shopping, the checkout line was long and slow. The clerk in our line was apparently new, crowds were impatient, and the cocky young man ahead of us spoke his piece to the cashier: "Impossible! You are *so slow!*" Impulsively, I spoke to him. "She's new. She's doing her best." He replied, "I'm an engineer, and this is ridiculous!" Perhaps it was his graduation day and he felt proud and cocky. Equally proud and cocky, I said, "I'm a teacher, and I can wait!" But what I really meant was, "I'm a writer and excited about it!" I embarrassed myself.

(The Ninth edition of *A Critical Handbook of Children's Literature* was published in 2012.)

◙ College in Wartime ◙

The recent display of World War II memorabilia here at the Knolls aroused in me memories of that period in my college-centered life.

First of all, I remember our family at our usual Sunday evening activities—eating a casual supper, settling in for an evening of reading or homework, just the usual Sunday with school/winter activities. Dad turned on the big old Philco for the Sunday news. Suddenly he called out, "Listen! We're at *war!* Listen to this!"

We stood silent. President Roosevelt was speaking: "Day of Infamy!" I scarcely knew the meaning of the word. It was shocking. That's all I could understand. The next days melted into one another as little by little we learned what had happened. War! Much would change. My college classmates would be going to war. We all watched and wondered who would be going where, what would happen, how we would manage. Brother Bob was a senior scheduled for graduate school at Syracuse University. Would he still go? Would all my male classmates go? When? Would war matter to me? I was just a girl, and probably nothing special would be expected of me.

At Concordia, questions seemed unspoken and yet they filled the air with uncertainty. Classes went on. News continued to fill the airwaves. In the Moorhead Theatre where usually we'd wait for the pre-show comedy, or for coming attractions, we began to see war news. A new word became significant: "The draft." Who would go? We continued to write our papers, to do our homework, to wonder and to question. Boys would fight—scary thought. What would be asked of girls? How could we help?

In the blur of those first weeks and months, we could do little but wonder, but bit by bit, the College made plans. Before long we knew about War Bonds, although probably few of our parents had money beyond tuition. We learned about saving anything metal—even those shiny Juicy Fruit gum wrappers? Rationing meant our mothers watched their ration stamps—so many points for a pound of ground beef! Macaroni and cheese again tonight?

We wore drab Army reject jackets, perhaps to feel "a part of it all." We'd just discovered elegant but affordable nylon hose, and now, when a run ruined a stocking, we saved it for the recycle box on the stair landing at the dorm. Nylon was re-used for parachutes, while we went back to wearing heavy rayon hose. Some of us joined the community women rolling bandages in church basements. The large Scandinavian population of Fargo-Moorhead was well aware of the Nazi takeover in Norway, and we young knitters joined a project called "Knitting for Norway." Bundles of drab khaki yarn complete with instructions for sweaters size 42 and over appeared in the girls' dorms. Heavy woolen sweaters we knitted were shipped to the small and overwhelmed Norwegian Army. (There *was* something we could do.)

Sweaters were easy, but trigger finger mittens took some tricky doing and only a few girls took them on. They involved four needles, a cuff, a smooth part, an opening for a thumb extension, another extended bit for the trigger finger, and another for the remaining three fingers. Then each of the three segments was finished. For the campus War Effort, I completed many trigger finger mittens, organized the bandage rollers, collected the donated nylons, set up salvage plans, and anything else we could think of doing.

Meanwhile the boys began to enlist. Some were pre-seminary students and were offered delays till graduation; a few took them and graduated at the expected time. My own special friend Don enlisted in the Marines. One of his older brothers went to war beside his Annapolis classmates; the other enlisted in the Army. Both were killed. Don returned to finish college and law school at the University of North Dakota.

As for me and my friends, Concordia College became a "girls' school." We gathered in groups, learned to bowl, and worried and hoped for the best for our classmates, waiting for the time when we could *rejoice*.

◘ A Prairie Ingenue Emigrates ◘

When senior year rolled round at Concordia College, I wondered, "What'll I do next?" Should I teach in a tiny North Dakota town? Or a Minnesota town, a bit bigger?" Mother, who had grown up in Pelican Rapids, MN, had taught in her hometown. Needing money for her final year at St. Olaf, she took a year off to earn money. Encouraged as she had been by Pelican's superintendent to go to college, the school administration must have been happy to get her application. In 1912 two years of college qualified one to teach, and she may have taught French or German. A year later she returned to St. Olaf to graduate. As a child I was intrigued by finding *Sartor Resartus* by Thomas Carlyle and a novel in German by Thomas Mann. Were they texts for college, Pelican Rapids, or her first real job in Thief River Falls, MN?

I heard a few tales (and wish I'd heard more) about how carefully the town observed a schoolteacher. She lived in a local home, so the town knew how, where, when and with whom her life developed. Having substitute taught for a few weeks in Pelican during my senior year, I found Mom's description accurate and unappealing for 1944. In those few weeks, I had seen no movie theatre, for example, and although they didn't actually roll up the sidewalks at dusk, the bakery was the only place open after 8 PM.

On the other hand, I'd loved college classes. Bob had gone off to Maxwell Graduate School of Public Administration at Syracuse. Perhaps I should try graduate school. Since I'd been an intercollegiate debater and *ex temp* competitor, as well as having acted in several plays, I'd see what was available in that general area. After seeking recommendations from three professors for my file, I combed the graduate school catalogs, focusing, I'll admit, on those far from Fargo: Universities of Wisconsin, Louisiana, Michigan, and Syracuse. Because of the war, applications were probably very few, and that accounted for several offers, including stipends and assistantships. I chose the best offer, Syracuse, the farthest from home, the biggest stipend, and site of Bob's graduate degree.

That same 1940 spring, a Concordia friend had been accepted at Syracuse for graduate work to become a Dean of Women. Surely North Dakota born-and-bred Ollie would be as excited as I was to explore the world. Would she go with me, take the Greyhound to Detroit, sail across Lake Erie to Buffalo on a cargo ship, and arrive in Syracuse by train? I thought it sounded pretty exciting, but she must have been reluctant: She often referred to our trip as our "immigrant arrival."

To my surprise, The East in many ways was similar to home. New York State, in fact, was not paved from edge to edge! Unlike imagined enrollees from Outer Space, Syracuse students had eyes and ears in the right places, and the same number of limbs as people from Fargo. Furthermore, they spoke my language.

The University stipend was enough to let me live well. It paid my $200 tuition, and I could walk to campus from my $6 a week room. At the cafeteria, milk cost seven cents and coffee five. I learned to drink coffee.

Rebecca Lukens

✦ Living in the Big City ✦

Dear Edie,

How many years is it now? Since we enrolled at Concordia? It's—no, it can't be—1940 subtracted from 2011? It's 70 years. Just think. And we haven't changed a bit. Just as gorgeous. Just as graceful. Just as sharp. And even more stylish.

We suffered through a lot. And loved it. A commuter, I often begged to share your single bed at the dorm so I could taste dorm life. At least once we then sneaked out of the dorm and risked some kind of discipline. We had religion classes, and AKX, and football games, and we went bowling and signed fake names on the score sheet—because we didn't want to admit to the true scores Becky and Edie had bowled. And when you sang in the great Concordia choir I was so jealous. So I took voice lessons and at the recital, you charitably insisted I did *not* sound like I'd swallowed a fly.

We were shy about being good students, so we didn't go up to sit on the stage when they honored good students at morning Chapel service. We just hid in the audience and were even more embarrassed to be called up separately to tromp across the stage in our twin Army surplus jackets.

Then, of course, when we graduated in 1944 and the war was on, we offered our remarkable services to President Brown to travel

North Dakota and Minnesota as recruiters for the next year's Concordia freshman class—which the war meant would be short of men and needing "girls." We traveled the states by Greyhound, stayed in Lutheran homes, and in an occasional scuzzy hotel. But because *you* knew about nutrition, we ate sensibly!

You left to teach music for a year, and we next joined forces with Gen on East 66th Street in New York City where we set the Big Town on fire, buying hats in a second-hand store on Second Avenue, people-watching in Central Park, going to the opera, and to every Broadway show we could get into for two dollars and twenty cents. And you met Lloyd, and I met Randy, and we each got married and had four kids apiece, you in Texas and I in Ohio.

Until the brilliant idea of traveling to London erupted. Once again we met in New York, then flew off for another Big City. Where once again we set the place on fire, from the botanical gardens to Westminster Abbey. And we sampled our first Indian food.

Now we are comfortably settled where we don't have to shovel snow or trim the spirea bushes or even vacuum the carpet, and I, at least, have forgotten how to cook. In fact, my cooking skills have not improved beyond our New York Jello chocolate pudding and the essential wire scouring ball for the burned pan. (When I left after our year as an apartment threesome, your good-bye gift was a package of pudding and a big red scouring pad.

Gen claimed malnutrition from that year, but I wouldn't have missed it for anything.)

Love,
Becky

Rebecca Lukens

❧ Andy's Very Best ❧

I'm sorry I had so few chances to watch Tom and Jean's Andy and Quinn, as well as Jim and Meg's Kat grow up. It's just a simple matter of geography. But I recall a Christmas I spent in California with Tom's young family.

We went out for a ride in early evening—for the traditional drive to "see-the-Christmas-lights." The boys were singing Christmas carols— and they knew a lot of them—to keep high the holiday spirit in the car. Andy, big brother to Quinn, was leading the sing-along as we drove past house after house. Inevitably Andy ran out of carols.

But not to be stopped by having reached the end of his reper-toire, Andy made up some new ones. We adults chuckled. But we shouldn't have. Quinn reminded us, "He's doing his very best."

Rebecca Lukens

◙ Gifts: Successful and Un-◙

Some gifts are flops. Some gifts are successes. Is there any way to predict success or failure? I wish I knew. Perhaps if I write about some successful ones, the reasons will appear.

Begin way back when I was little. Having a birthday on December 27, just two days after Christmas, meant that if long-awaited Christmas Eve brought some quiet disappointment, there was always the chance that Birthday Day would make up for it. The Christmas I was five and brother Bob was seven, he got a bicycle. A *bicycle!* Up the hill to visit the kids there! Around the block! To faraway places he hadn't seen except from the car! He'd find more friends besides the ones next door! If Mom and Dad let him, he could see the world! They must have known that.

I looked at my gift. They'd chosen a picture for my bedroom wall, a picture of a little Dutch girl with a white turned-back cap and wooden shoes. What would I do with that? Look at it in the morning when I woke up. Then get dressed as usual. The Dutch girl would just hang there all day, until the next morning when I woke up. Perhaps Birthday Day on the 27th would be better.

They tried. Mom and my two loving aunts. It was a doll. "A beautiful doll," they called it. And it was beautiful. Blonde hair, real hair, even. But what do you *do* with a doll? You admire it, and carry it around. You dress it—but it was already dressed. You put it to bed. It lies there. You could give it a name. Why? It was just a doll, and couldn't talk back. And it certainly couldn't explore the universe! I wasn't the only disappointed person; Mom felt it, too. I hope I didn't sulk and fume although I'm sure I begged for a chance to ride Bob's bike. But my legs were too short to reach the pedals. Later, ages later, I would get a used bike, all dinged-up and painted by Dad just like Bob's, but a girls' version. It could take me around the block and anywhere else. Sadly, however, my memory of that Christmas is clouded by my memory of Mom who was sad to have disappointed me.

When Ruthie and I got a bit older, we tried to surprise Dad and Mother at gift time. Once we bought Dad a puppy for his birthday. (Suspect no selfish motives, please.) It was not a big hit. Perhaps we were trying to replace our beloved cocker spaniel that had fallen through the ice in the close-by Red River? But the puppy soon lived elsewhere, permanently, with Dad's golfing partner.

More successful were the individually embroidered and auto-graphed ("From Becky" on one leg and "From Ruthie" on the other) wool hunting socks we knit, mine for his left leg and hers for the right. Mom loved books. I well remember discovering my first used book store. I bought her a slightly worn volume, its pages a bit gray and tired looking. She pretended to love it. But for another Christmas, the ruffled blouse was more successful.

Later on I wondered what to get for my nieces and nephews who lived abroad, in that romantic city called Geneva. The Swiss Army knife for my nephew was a hit, but every kid he knew had one, bought right there around the corner in Switzerland. Once, appalled at the haul my kids had collected in their Halloween trick-or-treat bags, I confiscated part of it—the part they least enjoyed, of course—and shipped it off with the Christmas gift box. Surprise! Success! Those poor chocolate-stuffed Geneva cousins loved the corn candy. That was perhaps the year I was so intrigued by the advent of American packaged mixes—brownies and chocolate cake and banana bread ready to mix and bake—that I loaded the box and paid more for the postage than for the gifts themselves.

I've written about the twin gold earrings Janie and Sally gave me one year, one for Christmas, the other for my birthday. I love them still. None of my ideas, however, exceeded Dad's delight when he found my tie-tac gift in his stocking. Apparently he'd always wanted a tie-tac that resembled a button, one that looked like he'd buttoned his tie to his shirt. Knowing Dad, he probably wore it to court to charm the judge.

When our own children were small and money was tight, my effort to make the pile of gifts under the tree seem bountiful fooled no one. Sometimes, the bright package contained disappointing socks and shirts and sweaters— although the corduroy cowboy suit with flaring chaps, and the Superman sweatshirt were hits. At least one package was always a "fun gift." Games. Puzzles. Inevitably books. Kits for making things. Sports equipment. One Christmas Eve Jim wore his football helmet to bed.

A recipe for successful gifts, anyone? I have none.

◙ Mom's Address Book ◙

Employment was very uncertain for the Lukens family. When I inherited Mom's address book, I noted a full page of Lukens addresses, a total history of our moves from one state to another, one house to another. Some addresses were only valid for a few months, as we waited for a house we were intending to move into as soon as it was available. Finally, we did manage to live at one address for eight long years. Incredible.

Obviously, some of these addresses were within a single town, but some were moves required by job changes, some changes of our own volition, and others the result of City Council action. We began in Albany with the State of New York, then for a career change, moved to Escanaba, MI, where Randy was for two years Assistant to the City Manager. Then a move to become a City Manager in Fairborn, OH, where we lived for six years as the small town adjacent to Wright-Patterson Air Force Base grew into a city inhabited by officers and civilians at the base. Mom added three new Lukens/ Fairborn addresses to her book.

Despite Randy's award as Man of the Year, we moved on to Troy, MI. The city was thirty-six square miles of farmland, and we settled for several months in Birmingham while our tract house was built: two addresses for just one move. In Troy, resistance was strong among the rural citizens who were reluctant to become a city, and in two years they voted for a mayor-council government. We were on our way once again.

This time, in Chillicothe, OH, Randy was again the first City Manager working with citizens dubious about becoming a "city" managed by a professional manager. First, we had an upstairs apartment in an old Victorian house on Water Street, close to the city park. Then we bought a lovely tri-level on Reservoir Hill above the old Southern-style city. Within five years, voters chose to return to their former mayor-council government. We left that beloved house on a hill.

Once again, the Lukens family was job hunting, and this time a city with a long history of city-manager government offered Randy a job. We moved to a comfortable home in Hamilton, OH, where we all lived and thrived until Randy resigned after five stressful years. His next job was in the land acquisition department of Champion Paper. When that division moved to Texas, Randy tried real estate sales, and with little success.

By now Jim, Tom, and Janie had left for college. It was departure time for Sally who had been accepted at Earlham College in Richmond, IN, and there was an offer for Randy at a development firm in Indianapolis. We bought a house there; I rented a room in Oxford and continued to teach at Miami on a full schedule set up over a three-day week. A new address for the two of us, and an additional one in Oxford for my room during the school week were added to Mom's little book

But not for long. Randy was forced into job hunting once again. He took a job in Ohio state government and moved into a Columbus apartment (another address in Mom's book) where we lived together from Thursday evening to Monday evening, when I once more drove off to Oxford. When the Democrats were voted out in Ohio state government, the Republican party chose new people for Randy's department, and we were once again hunting.

This time, the last address that listed us as Mr. and Mrs. C. R. Lukens, was Washington Blvd., Hamilton. Within a few months there—after totally renovating the tri-level home with the help of a Miami architect—our lives changed for good. It was at this time that my Dad, who had always been there to assist us if we needed it, died. I felt lost without the psychological and financial security Dad had provided, and again Randy was job hunting. I remained the sole breadwinner again, and stayed so until he was hired by the City of Hamilton, moved into an apartment, and ultimately a house of his own.

Rebecca Lukens

◉ Emergency One ◉

All this time, while Mom was adding one address after another to her little black book, Dad had been concerned: *Will they ever settle down?*

As a self-employed attorney, he was not eligible for the earliest form of Social Security, but when the law changed to allow him to contribute to SS, he began to receive a small check, one he felt he had not really earned. Each month his Social Security check went into a checking account called "Emergency Fund"; each of his three children had withdrawal access when an emergency arose.

To us it was a "sacred trust," no silly whims or luxuries, but at one point I did withdraw enough for Randy to register with a search agency that advertised as a placement source for professionals. Our two thousand dollar Emergency Fund fee brought no job offers, and Randy next took a brief job with a developer in Indianapolis. I continued to teach a full load at Miami in three days, and commuted Monday nights to Oxford, returning to Indianapolis on Thursday evening. After our brief stay, Randy got a Columbus political appointment working for the State of Ohio. Mom added a Reynoldsburg, Ohio, address to her little black book.

Several more Lukens's addresses were written in the little address book, all in Mom's nearly illegible "backhand" script. But one day when things were fairly stable for us, I suggested to my siblings that we buy a small sailboat for all our progeny to use when we were visiting Pelican Lake, Minnesota, in the summertime. We'd use the Emergency Fund for money, and call our little Sunfish "Emergency One." Ruthie and Bob were in total agreement. "Scary idea! Not a real emergency. Can't do it.... Fun, though.... You do it."

So I did. Ordered it. Had it delivered. Bought little rubber stick-on letters that spelled EMERGENCY ONE, and left for Pelican Lake.

Dad was surprised. A bit disgruntled. But when he saw how his grandchildren loved it, he, too, settled down to enjoy watching them enjoy EMERGENCY ONE.

◙ Alone in the Algerian Market ◙

In Luxemburg for a semester of leave, I rented a room with Mme. Dumont, owner of a notorious Basset Hound. Mme. worked for Luxair, and was sure she could find me the perfect package for a visit to Spain. Go for it, I said.

I disembarked in Torremolinos, a jumping city that to me resembled a tawdry replica of Miami Beach at its worst. My package "room" turned out to be an apartment that slept six, and I was alone in an impersonal and sterile looking house. On the streets, people, people everywhere. Tourist ads. Commodities of all kinds— "Leather goods at bargain prices." This wasn't what I had had in mind for a trip to Spain and its blooming olive trees. To block out my disappointment and take a break from puzzling over what to do about it, I took a nap. My motto: *When life overwhelms, go to sleep.*

On awakening, I locked up my castle and moseyed over to a tourist shop with my single question: "How do I get out of here?" There were many possibilities for day trips as well as longer absences. I chose a bus ride to Algeciras, a city on the tip of Spain at the Strait of Gibraltar; I'd get a room chosen from my copy of *Europe on $10 a Day* and from there I'd venture to Africa. Imagine it! Africa! Obviously, no plush appointments could be found for $10, so I shouldn't have been surprised when the clerk welcomed this wide-eyed American with a heavy skeleton key—like the key that opened outhouses on Pelican Lake, MN. But I was off to Africa.

At the ferry dock, I was approached by a man I assumed was an Arab; he wore a long black robe, a cylindrical red hat, and those shoes with heels folded over and curly, pointed toes. "Alone, are you?" he asked. "Want to go over to Algiers?" He named a reasonable price for my phony money, and I agreed to the ferry ride with the "rest of his group," which turned out to be me.

From the ferry I saw the Strait, and that huge rock called Gibraltar; it looked just like the rock in the insurance ad. My tour of Algiers took me into a world I'd seen only in the movies: *Casablanca* in the flesh. Mobs of people. Narrow streets. Stands called shops. Piles of strange-looking merchandise—none of which aroused in me an overwhelming need. After a thorough tour, the guide stopped to chat at length with the proprietor of a tea stand; I never did like tea, but I, of course, needed tea. More money than I thought reasonable changed hands—but what did I know about the tea market? My guide spoke to the shop owner with lavish gestures. I imagined his apology: "Next time, I bring many more."

Next came the *big* shopping stop. He confidently stopped at a huge market with stall after stall of merchandise for tourists, none of it necessary for my happiness. His first stop was to fulfill my assumed need for a "Persian" rug. The vendor unrolled one monstrous carpet after another, incredulous that I needed nothing like it. It wasn't the size. Nor the price. ("Very good bargain," I was told.) It was something neither vendor nor guide could believe: I just wasn't interested. Much verbiage, many gesticulations, so I bought a pair of those down-at-the-heel, pointy-toed shoes in their most monstrous size.

My guide was puzzled: Why was I unaffected by the prices he had found for me? "I'm not rich," I said. "How can you be poor? You are a teacher," he said "Teachers don't make much money," I explained. "How can that be? Americans are rich." I had no answer to that one, but stumbled through a nonsensical answer: "There are so many educated people in the U.S." What had that to do with school levies?

We stopped for lunch at an elegant restaurant, where I sat on the floor, on a soft, colorful cushion beside a low table. More Monopoly money changed hands. Who knew what our two meals cost? Much unintelligible conversation, and we were off to the ferry landing, where I think I tipped him generously. I next counted my remaining cash and tried bargaining with the ubiquitous vendors. Aboard the ferry, I at least knew my white dress decorated with machine embroidery in bright green (a jalapa, perhaps?) was cotton, not the "silk" a heavily laden tourist bragged about. I knew rayon when I saw it.

I'd been to Africa.

❧ The Caregiver ❧

My phone rang one Sunday afternoon. It was granddaughter Andrea.

"Nana, have you thought about visiting Grandma Jane?" she asked.

"Yes, I have," I said, "but in the snow I'm not sure I can manage the parking lot steps." Andrea immediately volunteered to come to pick me up for the trip to McCullough-Hyde Hospital. It turned out to be a moving experience.

Andrea parked close to the hospital entrance, and immediately offered me her arm for the trip in to see Jane Gross. She knew where to find the elevators, and where to turn right, then left when we got to our floor. On Andrea's arm, I followed her to an open doorway across from the nurse's station. "We have to wear gowns. So we don't bring germs into Grandma's room." She found me a gown, held it for me, and tied the strings at my neckline.

"Don't wake Grandma. I want to do that," Andrea said, and walked to the far side of the bed. Gently she patted Jane's arm. "Grandma, I have a surprise for you. Another visitor. It's your friend Becky." As Jane's eyes fluttered open, she recognized me and smiled a welcome. In a minute or two Andrea reminded Jane that her own brother from Manhattan had also visited. And that the uncles and aunts and California cousins had visited a few days earlier. She added a note of how glad they all were to see her.

"Your lunch is here, Grandma. Do you want to eat? I'll help." But Jane had slid down in her elevated bed, so Andrea, once she realized she couldn't push Jane up without help, touched Jane's call button. A nurse appeared immediately, left for another nurse to help, and together the two of them pulled their patient up from her slumped position so she could eat. Before the nurses left the room, Andrea asked, " I can't stay very long. When I have to leave, can you find someone to feed Grandma the rest of her lunch?" They could.

Quickly and efficiently Andrea next pushed the bedside table into place so Jane could see her dinner as Andrea counted it all out: "You have chicken and mashed potatoes and peas and a dish of fruit. Can I help you with it? And here's a drink. Shall I hold it for you?"

Carefully Andrea cut up the fruit, telling Jane about each bite: "Here's a little piece of apricot…. And this is half a strawberry…. Want a slice of peach? Now another bit of chicken."

With her eye on the clock, Andrea said to me, "I have to be at Talawanda at three o'clock for choir rehearsal. So we can't stay long." But she continued feeding Jane until I began to worry about her schedule. But not Andrea, who was in charge. "We have to go now, Grandma, but the nurse promised she'd see that you got your lunch."

I removed my gown, rolled it up, and Andrea tucked it into the laundry basket. In the hall outside Jane's room, she lingered at the nurses' station, reluctant to leave until she was certain that Grandma

Jane would have her lunch. When the nurse reappeared and Andrea heard her reassuring, "We'll take care of her," Andrea finally took my arm and we left for the elevator.

From home I later called my daughter Sally. I wiped away my tears as I glowed about her seventeen-year-old caregiver, her daughter Andrea.

Rebecca Lukens

🔲 My Life As an Oil Baroness 🔲

It didn't last long. A matter of minutes, actually. I answered the phone, answered the question, and it began. "Rebecca Johnson Lukens? Sister of Robert Johnson? I'm Mr X, agent for Diamond Resources in Williston, North Dakota. I'd like to talk to you about the oil rights you own."

Immediately I perked up. "I've had two or three other inquiries about North Dakota oil rights, but when my Dad's trust was settled, I believe the Fargo bank took care of that, too." But this call was from Williston, ND and I had just read an article in *The New Yorker* about the hundreds of oil derricks around Williston. I'd better listen.

My caller began to enlighten me. "Perhaps you don't know that when land is sold, that sale does not include underground mineral rights."

Surprised, I admitted my ignorance. "Dad was an attorney and the vice consul for Norway in North Dakota. I remember that, since he began his practice during the Depression, he often took as an attorney's fee an odd piece of property. Like, for instance, a used car, our first radio, a piano, or supplies of vegetables, eggs, or chickens. Perhaps he got the oil rights as an attorney's fee. As a matter of fact, I do recall his chuckling once: 'Imagine it! Whoever thinks there might be oil in North Dakota! Nothing but prairie, oats, barley, and wheat. That's North Dakota.'"

The agent, went on to say that Bob and I owned oil rights for two and a third acres. Diamond Resources was offering me $2,300, or $1000 an acre. Bob had died some time ago, but his three children—Mark, Eric and Hilary—would get half of that big twenty-three hundred dollars. My half would go into my trust: One thousand one hundred and fifty dollars. Later, when split four ways for Jim, Tom, Jane, and Sally, each check would amount to $287.50.

Oil Dividends Worth Framing. I think I'll mail each of them a check for $287.50, framed. That's big stuff! They'll all be oil barons, Captains of Industry.

Dear Family Four:

Today I saw Jim Robinson, my attorney, who had by now read the proposal sent by the oil company agent. I'd been wrong. First of all, Diamond Resources would make the same offer to Bob's heirs. And, more importantly, the offer was for a five-year lease on oil rights, and if the well produced, there would be annual income. The lease would be renewable for three additional years. So I said, "Go!" And signed the agreement. Maybe there will be a few shekels for my trust—and for my four heirs.

With love from your Speculator-Mother

7/2/2011

I have just learned that the oil is to be found by "fracking"—environmentally destructive. What I read from the oil companies is highly defensive. Now I feel doubtful.

~M

❧ Never Too Late ❧

Not long ago here at the Knolls we heard a speaker from the Miami University gerontology program whose topic was the nature of dementia and of Alzheimer's Disease. The room was full, each of us worried about the same issues: "Me? Which one? Neither? Both?" We listened and we learned. Here and there some of us were alarmed. Others were reassured. But then one listener asked the question, "How do I recognize symptoms in my Great Aunt Ellen?" (For me and my cohort, a great aunt is sufficiently remote in age to serve as a comfortable example.)

The reply scared me into partial paralysis. "If Great Aunt Ellen has always been a methodical person, examine her check register. Are there deletions, cross-outs, or repetitions? That might tell."

I envisioned my check register. It was filled with deletions, cross-outs, and repetitions. Suddenly alert, I thought, "I must get out of here. Run home, make a few alterations before anyone finds out."

No point in immediate examination of the check register itself. Memory now was strong. Just go and find a new, unused check register in the desk drawer. Ah, found one. Brand new and clean. Open it to its center, the place where the staples split the center pages. Jerk out that virginal double page. Open it, and ignoring the old blacked-out entries of the used check register, copy only the line that should have been entered correctly in the first place. Check dates and numbers. Recalculate dollar amounts. Note the beauty of the new register pages.

How to disguise the new pages as originals? Search for Scotch tape, then affix the sparkling new pages over the formerly offending ones. Perfect. I'm a meticulous record keeper once again. True, daughter Sally, my estate administrator, may wonder about all that Scotch tape. It's never too late.

✿ Anniversary of the Fall ✿ of the Berlin Wall

The Berlin Wall, a strange thing to catch my eye in the morning paper, and yet I do have strong memories of that monstrosity.

In January of 1980 I had an appointment as Resident Scholar at the Luxembourg campus of Miami University, my first and only sabbatical. I'd submitted the required proposal, written to prove I had a research project in mind. Related to my textbook, *A Critical Handbook of Children's Literature*, the proposal was an inquiry into what U.S. children's literature was translated into European languages and read by European children.

The first checkpoint was, of course, the library of Luxembourg City. My next stop was London, and I recall vividly how impressed I was with the availability of children's books in British bookstores. The U.S. books, however, were not contemporary, not what U.S. children were reading, but books from earlier days, infrequently read by today's American children: *The Leatherstocking Tales* of the American frontier written by James Fenimore Cooper, and tales of the wilderness enlivened by Jack London's *The Call of the Wild*. Such a world of frontier and wilderness must seem fascinating to Europe's long civilized and cultivated world.

Berlin seemed the next closest stop for my search, so off I went by train. Once settled in a Berlin bed-and-breakfast (I locked myself out by getting back late one evening, but awakened my angry host and was somehow excused), I went in search of the State Library. Since it was in East Berlin, and thus under Soviet control, I would have to go through Checkpoint Charlie. A cab dropped me off at a small, temporary-looking building surrounded by barbed wire, and there I joined other visitors waiting on a bench. As I looked around at them, they seemed ordinary people—a mother and a daughter, and another small family, all wanting to go to specific addresses, the homes of friends, grandparents or other family members they hoped to visit.

Once the line led me to the barred window at the counter, the uniformed guard asked me to show my identification, my passport. He opened it to my picture, and moving his eyes back and forth, back and forth, from my face to my picture, apparently satisfied that I was indeed who I claimed to be. He then let me through the locked gate into East Berlin on the other side of the fence.

I easily found the State Library, a castle on the broad through-way of central Berlin, the street called Unter den Linden, memorialized from newsreel pictures of crowds during World War II. It was an intimidating sight. The library was a vast gray castle behind a heavy iron fence nearly concealed by tall shrubs; it made me question the importance of my errand. Although far from inviting, the open gate was not threatening, so I walked cautiously down the long walkway to the castle doors, up the many broad stone steps and into the majestic hall. The uniformed guard there asked about my mission, and I said I wanted to see the children's library. He pointed me to another uniformed guard at the hall counter; there I uneasily left my purse, my coat, and my precious American passport.

The Children's Room was on the second floor, accessible by means of a twelve-foot wide series of marble steps gracefully winding up into the atmosphere. There, at the top, I found the Children's Room, and beyond the double doors stood a lectern. When I stopped to note the journal outspread there, I was met by the only article I had ever sent to an international journal. My interest in feminism had prompted me to survey U.S. children's stories looking for books with girls as protagonists, central to the plot; confirming my expectations, there were very few. I'd sent the article to the UNESCO journal, and there it was—open before me in the German State Library.

Once again I had to identify myself. My German was non-existent, but by excitedly pointing alternately to myself and to the article, I managed to convince the librarian that I was who I was. She seemed as delighted as I.

My enthusiasm, certainly not my German, must have conveyed somehow the reason for my being there in her library, because she graciously led me to the shelves where I found American children's stories in German translation.

But first I stopped to admire the row of books about the Indians of North America, written by a 19th century German named Karl May who had never visited the exotic American places he described. "Children love these," the librarian said. And, of course, Jack London and James Fenimore Cooper were there. I nodded gratefully at *The Call of the Wild*, and *The Leatherstocking Tales*, and saluted Natty Bumppo, stalker of American Indians.

The Birth of Women's Studies at Miami

In the early Seventies, Professor Millie Seltzer was appointed Associate Provost at Miami, and some things began to change.

Professor Seltzer developed a non-credit Continuing Education class on women's issues. A series of evening lectures focused on women in a variety of situations: women and aging, women in politics, women in the workplace, women in advertising, women and child care, literature by and about women, and the portrayal of girls in literature for children.

Lecturers enjoyed the experience of talking with adult women eager to listen and respond. One professor developed a class about women in literature for Continuing Education. In five weeks, women read five novels, beginning with *The Awakening* by Kate Chopin, published in 1899. The controversial novel explored the creative, maternal, professional and sexual awakening of the protagonist. Its publication had once been a breakthrough for women who had been reading only about the lives of men in fiction, or the lives of women in "women's magazines." The class discussed this first novel with avid interest and went on to four more-recent ones.

The two English professors leading the class realized that there was a world of interest out there, and developed a class for their department. At the time, the College of Arts and Science was feeling threatened by the overwhelming popularity of the School of Business, and was eager to offer classes with new appeal. The new course was listed under the general category "English 201, Popular Literature," and was aimed at non-scholarly readers, those who read for pleasure and interest.

The search for a suitable Women's Studies textbook began. Very few were available. The most popular literature text, *Images of Women in Literature*, showed women primarily as related to men: as unpleasant bitches, controlling wives, passive objects. Such negative portrayals forced the two professors to search for more positive yet realistic selections. Plans for a new anthology began. In 1978, D.C. Heath published *Woman: An Affirmation*, edited by Professors Fannin, Lukens, and Mann. Its sections followed the chronological order of women's lives.

Meanwhile, a Political Science professor ran for the Ohio legislature, and with this experience behind her, offered a class called "Women in Politics." Classes in other departments followed: Sociology, Psychology, Religion, Gerontology, Philosophy, and History. To general surprise, a male professor in the School of Business also saw a new market, and developed a class about women in administration.

Miami was not alone. University programs and classes develop not only from the need to educate students about life and careers, but also from the need for warm bodies in the classroom. Throughout higher education, women had been discovered as a source of departmental revenue. With the support of Miami's Provost, the Women's Studies program was cross-listed with the departments offering the classes. It became obvious that Miami had the beginnings of a program and needed an introductory class called "Introduction to Women's Studies." Such a class was soon developed.

It wasn't an easy beginning. The Oxford *Press* soon published a "Letter to the Editor" from an English professor protesting that women were already acknowledged in literature. His letter was followed the next week by three letters from his department colleagues who believed the new classes were legitimate. Women students had long been reading the writings of men, whose primary subjects were men. Women were not wholly like men, but had experiences of their own that contribute to human understanding.

In fact, Women's Studies programs began with professional women who knew that their lives were not identical to those of men, and wanted their insights and experiences to be acknowledged and understood. The program grew with the help of enthusiastic students and faculty as well as support from Miami administration. In February of 2005, Women's Studies hosted an international symposium on gender, race, class, and sexuality.

Vignettes of early experience

With new legitimacy, Miami women began to change. One WMS/ Psychology professor visited her gynecologist for her annual Pap test. When the bill came, it was addressed to her husband; she doubted that he had had a Pap test and so cleared up the confusion by writing the check to the physician's wife. The indomitable Millie Seltzer, meeting a new oncologist, was greeted by the doctor: "And how are we doing today, Millie?" Millie responded with, "You may call me Doctor Seltzer. Unless, of course, you'd like me to call you 'Bobbie.'"

The Women's Center organized an awareness program, asking campus women to submit brief anecdotes describing situations in which they had felt discrimination. These short, written incidents were then hung by clothespins from a line strung between the trees on Slant Walk. My story was about being singled out in a graduate class and asked, "Is this clear to the girl from North Dakota?" We were all "girls" at that point, so I thought nothing of it at the time. (Besides, I was used to being thought of as a western barbarian.)

In an early Introduction to Women's Studies class, a woman student, the first woman appointed to Miami's Security staff, reported one morning that she had just arrested a campus rapist. Another student left in tears: the arrested man was her roommate's boyfriend.

In a full session, the university Faculty Senate addressed the proposal that department heads be addressed as "chairs" rather than "chairmen." Loud protests arose from that august body: "Ridiculous! A chair is a piece of furniture!" The change was slow in coming, but it did happen. And to our surprise, appeals for salary equity were heard and acted upon.

As a female senior professor, I appeared before the Miami Board of Trustees in support of changing the words of our alma mater from "Men of Old Miami" to gender-inclusive terms. I suggested that even churches—churches being institutions highly reluctant to change—were adopting gender-inclusive language. A committee was appointed to "study" the issue. Some time later that minor change was accepted.

Miami was somewhat early in developing a Women's Studies program. After some time, the Director had a little released time for administration, and later the directorship became a half-time appointment. A Women's Center appeared on campus, a single room with a secretary and a library contributed by eager faulty. Finally, a full-time administrator was appointed.

On Looking Into Old Papers

This week, the week my self-published book arrived on my front porch—neatly wrapped, padded, and adequate in most ways—has been a return to traditional old lady behavior. I've been looking over old stuff that preceded other old stuff.

I have a folder of "poetry," so-called, written during my adolescence and filled with the sense of isolation common to that period of youth. It is sad to think those "serious" thoughts I was claiming as my own are so universally identified nowadays as being part of growing up. Could I really have included some of them in my application to graduate school? I'm tossing them out. Now.

Another "essay" in the file, called "Efficiency Expert," is based on a story my dad told us about the man who rented him an office in his Fargo law office suite. Pete Garborg, once his term in the North Dakota legislature began, was "too busy" to take care of his clients, so Dad took timely care of them. Finally he took over Pete's really wealthy ones—at their request, of course. The piece is based on facts, but the tone is my own adolescent effort at humor. I've done better.

The next ancient folder I found to be interesting. During my "Discovering Feminism" days, I read about the Women's Club movement, a revolution of sorts. Beginning in the 19th century, women, particularly educated women, were feeling there should be more to life than housekeeping; they began to gather in groups to talk about ideas other than their limited home lives. Women's clubs with the goal of self-development and social reform developed all over the country. In Fargo, North Dakota, such a group organized, and Mom was part of the Roundtable Study Club.

Mom was not only no crusader, but she was also very self-effacing, so I imagine her joining was through persuasion. The group included perhaps a dozen women, each one committed to "giving a paper" each year. When it was Mom's turn, she took her assignment very seriously. The dining room table was dedicated to her research and writing—for months, it seemed to me, although I doubt that. She agonized over her work, never thinking it was good enough or complete enough, always just a little short of the perfection she aimed for. One year the Roundtable Club must have delved into Art. Mom either chose or was assigned the topic of "The French Impressionists." The evidence in the paper is clear that when she chose to explore something, she "went at it hard" as she would have said. Another paper, one on "Miracle, Mystery and Morality Plays," also survives in this folder.

I have no record of the many talks Mom gave. She was continually surprised that people wanted to hear her "give a talk." And she prepared and prepared, even for the annual Mother-Daughter

Banquet held each spring at First Lutheran Church. As I recall, some bits might have come from that "old saw" master, Edgar Guest, sentimental and homey-sounding. Mom apparently knew her Mother-Daughter audience.

I remember one Mother-Daughter banquet at which two sisters played a piano duet. Suddenly the music stopped. "Where are you?" one sister snapped. "Right *there!*" growled the other sister as she pointed a sharp finger at the music. "Well, I'm *here*," the first sister snarled as she pointed at another spot. Then the climaxing horror. A word *we* never said at our house shattered the Mother-Daughter solemnity: the sister playing the bass end of the piano yelled: "Oh, you big snot!"

I probably gasped. But Mom kept her cool.

◙ My Version: The Knolls of Oxford ◙

I couldn't have imagined how well the Knolls would fit my retirement lifestyle. Miami University had been my working home since
1964, when I first began teaching in the Department of English—
and loving it.

Occasionally Department colleagues lunching together in the
1809 Room at the Shriver Center fantasized about retirement. We'd
like to stay in the small town of Oxford, the place that was quietly-
busy–if such a possibility exists–throbbing nine months of the
year with young people and action, things to hear and see, and old
friends to greet. But where would we live?

News went around that a new Continuing Care Community was
to be built west of Oxford, between Fairfield Road and Contreras.
We checked the rolling fields and wooded area, noted the small
stream that might become a pond, and cautiously the First Forty
put our money down.

Here there are congenial people, some who once were Miami
students, others whose children are Miami alumni or have settled as
adults in the Tri-State area. Contemporaries all. With the able care
of the staff, we are "taken care of" in every way. Grounds are beau-
tifully maintained, and the social schedule could keep us busy every
day—if that's what we wanted. Cottages are complete and filled

with light; neighbors are friendly; nursing care is across the pond in the Commons, and all is well.

I no longer teach in the Women's Studies program or grade technical writing papers, but if I'm hungry for a class, I register for one in Miami's Institute for Learning in Retirement. And the 1809 Room in the Shriver Center is still there. Here at the Knolls, our retirement hopes are fulfilled.

◙ Words for My Sister's Funeral ◙

Ruthie's daughter Liv called me with the news. After several years with early-onset Alzheimer's Disease, her mother, my little sister Ruthie, had died. The funeral was to be in Minneapolis in three days. Could I come? And since she and her brothers Nord and Nathan could not agree on who of the three should speak for the family, would I please do that for them all? Of course I would.

As I sat on the plane headed for Minneapolis, I had time to think of what to say. After she retired as General Secretary of the World YWCA in Geneva, she and Arne had moved to Minnesota. Now I was glad that, for her family's sake, the end had finally come. But what could I say? My few hours of waiting and in flight left me to my very personal, sisterly memories, and I jotted down a few things.

Just yesterday I found in my files a copy of what I had put together mentally, then typed up at Ruthie's apartment on the morning of the funeral.

As I think of my sister, three major emotions come to mind— along with many others.

"The first of these is awe. She was awesome. She not only sang and played the cello, but she could dive! She was editor of the high school yearbook. She made top grades. Bob and I were good students, but somehow I knew I couldn't compare. She threw herself into every challenge. When one of our toughest Fargo High teachers saw her racing down the hall, walking at an angle as she always did—with her head forward and her feet hurrying behind—Miss Follett stopped her and said, 'Ruth, your head can't do anything till your feet get there.'

When I went to Europe and to Geneva for the first time, Ruthie went shopping with me. Using my high school French–taught to us at Fargo High by Miss Nilsen with her Norwegian lilt–Ruthie listened to my halting speech, and immediately interrupted. In rapid French, she said to the clerk, 'This is my sister from the States. I will speak for her.' And she did. Who knows what I might have bought without her?

And I thought of Ruthie with envy all those years as well. She made Phi Beta Kappa at St. Olaf College, though she graduated in three-and-a-half years. From Taipei, Taiwan, and from Geneva she wrote those long, fascinating letters, five or six pages, single spaced on onionskin paper, telling of the remarkable things she'd seen, the people she'd met, the dinners she'd hostessed, and the travels she'd fit into that remarkable schedule–to say nothing of the elaborate birthday parties she'd arranged for her children. I'd envy her–envy her energy, her enthusiasm, her imagination, and her opportunities. When I spoke of my reactions, she merely said, "Yes. But when Arne's off in some exotic place, and I'm alone in Geneva, it's no more exciting than Chillicothe, Ohio."

But over all, my thoughts turn to a third reaction: delight. How we laughed. I remember one morning when I came down to breakfast in Fargo and I returned Dad's greeting with that of a docile, eager-to-please child: "Good morning, Daddy!" But some minutes later, on her own schedule, Ruthie came down. "Good morning, Ruthie." Silence. Then louder. "Good morning, Ruthie." Silence. Then louder still, as though she hadn't heard. "Good morning, Ruthie!" And Ruthie answered with a thunderous, "All right then. Good morning." No "Daddy." No sweet docility. She spoke when she wanted to speak, and said what she wanted to say. I was awed, envious, and delighted.

Like most sisters, we had our own inside jokes, the ones about the elephant and the mouse*, and the baby ostrich**, and about family. About the visits from Mom's childhood friend Bessie from Pelican Rapids, who marked time by funerals: "Two funerals ago...." Time after time we collapsed in laughter. Before Ruthie started school—perhaps at five, or perhaps, knowing her, at a year-and-a-half—she wanted to know how to write. She began by learning how to print her own name: RUTHIE. Then, from the comics, she discovered a two-syllable word with only two letters: ANNA. And in the Popeye comics, Bluto was often felled by Popeye with a resounding PLOP! Another word Ruthie found she could write! She covered page after page with "RUTHIE ANNA PLOP. RUTHIE ANNA PLOP." From my more sophisticated vantage point, I was delighted.

At Pelican Lake, when our families could occasionally meet for a vacation, Ruthie and I often dissolved in uncontrollable laughter. During those dinner table conversations that sometimes lasted until time for the next meal, I once saw my older son Jim roll his eyes while we laughed. He said to his brother Tom, "What do you expect? They're sisters." Once when I visited her in New Jersey, we laughed so hard in the New York City subway station—our arms filled with newly purchased peacock feathers and other wonders—that we had to lean against the tiled wall and just hope we could recover enough to take the proper train back to Montclair.

Awe, envy, and delight. I have missed Ruthie during her last several years. Now I shall miss her even more."

Our inside jokes:

* The elephant one day looked down his trunk and discovered a mouse at his feet and said, "You are the tiniest and most insignificant thing in the whole wide world."
The mouse squeaked back, "I've been sick."

** The mother and father ostrich decided to hide from their offspring, so they put their heads in the sand. The baby ostrich woke up and asked, "Where *is* everybody?"

⊕ "Brothers are to help" ⊕

When Janie and Sally were little, I occasionally read to them a little picture book entitled *A Hole Is To Dig*, to a child a perfect description of the function of a hole. One page declared that "Brothers are to help." That page both girls vigorously rejected. They had never heard of nor experienced such a purpose for brothers. Their brothers Tom and Jim were to resist, demand, tease, make life difficult. Even jump out of dark places.

I thought back to the summer of 1940. When I was admitted to Concordia College, the admissions staff set up a welcoming party for incoming freshmen who lived in the area. I went, hoping to meet new classmates and perhaps even a few who were already students! Early the next week, I got a phone call. A college boy, a junior, wanted me to go to the movies with him! I would. When I hung up, I told my brother Bob the name of my Saturday date.

Bob groaned. "You're really going with *him*? Shall I get my gun?" True to form, this brother was *not* helping! Besides—Bob hadn't told me he'd sold his Model A Ford to my date! Date and I rattled off in that familiar old junker.

On May 14, 2011, Granddaughter Andrea was named Prom Queen at Talawanda High School. I was delighted. She's a gem.

I called. Congratulated both Andrea and her mother, Sally, and we glowed with pride. Next day, Sally called to tell me that Andrea's brother Daniel had bought flowers for his sister. The card read, "Congratulations! Don't fuck it up."

I called Andrea's Uncle Tom and told him the story. He roared! Brothers are to help!

Next day I was chatting with a retired colleague, and when I told him the stories, he told me one. When Hardy was in grad school, his mother called him in tears: "Your sister has fallen in love, and is getting married. They'll live in South Africa and I'll never see her again." Hardy said to his mom, "Just be glad she found *someone* to marry her."

Brothers are to help.

◉ With Apologies to Emily ◉

When I was a shy teenager, I memorized Emily Dickinson's poem.

I'm nobody.
Who are you?
Are you nobody, too?
Don't tell.
They'd banish us.

How dreary to be somebody,
How public like a frog
To tell one's name
The livelong day
To an admiring bog.

Rebecca Lukens

This is my current version:

How dull it is to be
The livelong day
Pre-occupied with Body—
Not with Mind.

Shall I stand?
Will I fall?
Can I reach my cane?
It's just a step away.
Or two...or more....

How's my pressure now?
Too high? Too low?
My head too light
To move from here to there?

Can I take my shower?
How will it be?
Too hot? Too cold?
Will I slip without my cane?
Can the grab bars hold?

Perhaps the bed
Is more secure.
But then—
Uncertainty once more.

I must not stay.
I'll only ask again:
"Shall I stand?
Suppose I fall.
Can I reach my cane?"

I pass the mirror and I ask,
"Who let Maude's mother in?
Please tell her
Not to come again."

She's spry. She's sharp. She's old.
And must be told
Unless she leans upon a cane,
She cannot come again.

Rebecca Lukens

❂ Bits of Nothing ❂

Yesterday when I parked at Walgreen's, I noticed a woman slowly backing herself out of the driver's side of her car, cane in one hand and a cast on one leg. Without giving it a thought, I said, "Can I help you?" She immediately replied, "You'd better help yourself." I waved my cane at her and smiled.

As I turned down an inner aisle in the store, I met her again and told her what I've said a hundred times: "When I began to carry a cane, I noticed that people came out of the woodwork to help me. I was shocked." She replied, "Oh, you didn't offend me. I just wish they'd told us that beforehand."

We wouldn't have dreaded our canes so much.

I stopped to see Sally, because I wanted her to put my electric toothbrush together properly. I told her that since I have no work to do, and nothing is expected of me—except just to show up—that I knew I had a tendency to repeat myself. I don't want to become a garrulous old woman who tells the same old thing over and over again, so I said, "When I start to repeat myself, Sally, will you please just say 'You already told me that.'"

Sally's instant comment: "You already told me that."

▣ About The Author ▣

Rebecca Lukens graduated with honors from Corcordia College in Moorhead, MN and earned an M.A. from Syracuse University. After working on the editorial staff of a children's encyclopedia in New York, she taught at St. Olaf College, New York State College, Albany, and later at Ohio University, Chillicothe.

She taught at Miami University in Oxford, OH from 1964-1987. Her classic textbook, *A Critical Handbook of Children's Literature*, now in its Ninth Edition (Allyn & Bacon, 2012) was first published by Scott Foresman in 1976. She is also the author of *A Critical Handbook of Literature for Young Adults*, published by Harper Collins in 1994. As well, Lukens co-edited a literature anthology, *Woman: An Affirmation*, published by D.C. Heath in 1979.

Since her retirement, she has taught in the Miami University Learning in Retirement program. She named her favorite class "Laughter: For Health and Sanity."

She has four children—Tom, Jim, Jane, and Sara—and six grand-children—Andrea, Daniel, Andy, Quinn, Rachel, and Kat.

⚜ Colophon ⚜

The text of this book is set in Centaur, a refinement of Roman inscriptional capitals designed by Bruce Rogers as a titling design for signage in the Metropolitan Museum. Rogers later designed a lowercase based on Nicolas Jenson's work from the mid-1460s, turning the titling into a full typeface.

The page corner ornament was selected from Lanston Typeface Corporation's Keystone Ornaments, a set of glyphs based on "running border" ornaments from the Keystone Type foundry of Philadelphia, circa 1903.

The fleuron to the side of each chapter heading is based on the design work of Charles Rennie Mackintosh.

Page margins were determined using the Van de Graaf canon.